Elements of Literature®

First Course

The Holt Reader

HOLT, RINEHART AND WINSTON

A Harcourt Education Company

Orlando • Austin • New York • San Diego • London

ISBN 978-0-03-099625-2
ISBN 0-03-099625-2

123456 179 11 10 09 08 07

Contents

To the Student

A Book for You

A book is like a garden carried in the pocket.
—Chinese Proverb

The more you put into reading, the more you get out of it. This book is designed to do just that—help you interact with the selections you read by marking them up, asking your own questions, taking notes, recording your own ideas, and responding to the questions of others.

A Book Designed for Your Success

The Holt Reader goes hand in hand with *Elements of Literature*. It is designed to help you interact with the selections and master important language arts skills.

The Holt Reader has three types of selections: literature, informational texts, and documents that you may encounter in your various activities. All the selections include the same basic preparation, support, and review materials. Vocabulary previews, skill descriptions, graphic organizers, review questions, and other tools help you understand and enjoy the selections. Moreover, tips and questions in the side margins ensure that you can apply and practice the skills you are learning as you read.

A Book for Your Own Thoughts and Feelings

Reading is about *you*. It is about connecting your thoughts and feelings to the thoughts and feelings of the writer. Make this book your own. The more you give of yourself to your reading, the more you will get out of it. We encourage you to write in this book. Jot down how you feel about the selection. Write down questions you have about the text. Note details you think need to be cleared up or topics that you would like to investigate further.

A Walk Through the Book

The Holt Reader is arranged in collections, just like *Elements of Literature*, the book on which this one is based. Each collection has a theme, or basic idea. The stories, poems, articles, or documents within the collection follow that theme. Let's look at how the arrangement of *The Holt Reader* helps you enjoy a collection as a whole and the individual selections within the collection.

Before Reading the Collection

Literary and Academic Vocabulary
Literary and academic vocabulary refers to the specialized language that is used to talk about books, tests, and formal writing. Each collection begins with the literary and academic terms that you need to know to master the skills for that collection.

Before Reading the Selection

Preparing to Read
From experience, you know that you understand something better if you have some idea of what's going to happen. So that you can get the most from the reading, this page previews the skills and vocabulary that you will see in the reading.

Literary Focus
For fiction selections—stories, poems, and plays—this feature introduces the literary skill that is the focus for the selection. Examples and graphic elements help explain the literary skill.

Reading Focus
Also in fiction selections, this feature highlights a reading skill you can apply to the story, poem, or play. The feature points out why this skill is important and how it can help you become a better reader.

Informational Text Focus
For informational, or nonfiction, selections, this feature introduces you to the format and characteristics of nonfiction texts. Those texts may be essays, newspaper articles, Web sites, employment regulations, application forms, or other similar documents.

Selection Vocabulary
This feature introduces you to selection vocabulary that may be unfamiliar. Each entry gives the pronunciation and definition of the word as well as a sentence in which the word is used correctly.

Word Study
Various activities reinforce what you have learned about the selection's vocabulary.

While Reading the Selection
Background gives you basic information on the selection, its author, or the time period in which the story, essay, poem, or article was written.

Side-Column Notes
Each selection has notes in the side column that guide your reading. Many notes ask you to underline or circle in the text itself. Others provide lines on which you can write your responses to questions.

A Walk Through the Book

Types of Notes

Several different types of notes throughout the selection provide practice for the skills introduced on the Preparing to Read pages. The notes help you with various strategies for understanding the text. The types of side-column notes are

- **Read and Discuss** notes ask you to pause at certain points so that you can think about basic ideas before proceeding further. Your teacher may use these notes for class discussions.
- **Literary Focus** notes practice the skill taught in the Literary Focus feature on the Preparing to Read page. Key words related to the specific skill are highlighted.
- **Reading Focus** notes practice the reading skill from the Preparing to Read page.
- **Language Coach** notes reinforce the language skill found in the Preparing to Read pages of *Elements of Literature*.
- **Vocabulary** notes examine selection vocabulary, academic vocabulary, and topics related to how words are used.

After Reading the Selection

Skills Practice

For some selections, graphic organizers reinforce the skills you have practiced throughout the selection.

Applying Your Skills

This feature helps you review the selection. It provides additional practice with selection vocabulary and literary, reading, and informational text focus skills.

After Reading the Collection

Skills Review

On the first page of the Skills Review, you can practice using the collection's academic vocabulary and selection vocabulary.

Language Coach

The second Skills Review page draws on the Language Coach skills in the *Elements of Literature* Preparing to Read pages. This feature asks you to apply those skills to texts from throughout the collection.

Writing Activity

You may have found that you need more practice writing. These short writing activities challenge you to apply what you have learned to your own ideas and experiences.

Oral Language Activity

Writing Activities alternate with Oral Language Activities. These features are designed to help you express your thoughts clearly aloud. The features are particularly helpful if you are learning English or if you need practice with Standard English.

Forms of Prose

Literary and Academic Vocabulary

---

interpret (IHN TUR PRIHT) *v.:* decide on the meaning of something.

She would interpret the invitation as a sign of friendship.

impact (IHM PAKT) *n.:* powerful effect.

The author's incredible images have an impact on readers.

insight (IHN SYT) *n.:* power to understand.

The author's story gives readers insight into the experience of adjusting to the customs of two cultures.

significance (SIGH NIHF UH KUHNS) *adj.:* importance; meaning.

Many of the events found in history textbooks are of great significance.

novel (NAH VUHL) *adj.:* a long piece of fiction.

When you read a novel, you are likely to encounter many characters, subplots, and conflicts.

biography (BY AHG RUH FEE) *n.:* the story of a real person's life.

The biography of the writer helped me to understand the real-life origins of some of the characters in her books.

Amigo Brothers

by Piri Thomas

LITERARY FOCUS: THE SHORT STORY

Most television shows are only a half-hour or an hour long. Because TV shows don't have as much time to develop a story as full-length movies do, their plots and conflicts tend to be less involved or complicated. The same is true when you compare short stories and novels. A **short story** is usually between five and twenty pages long, whereas a novel is usually more than one hundred pages long. Although short stories and novels may have identical plot patterns, such as the one shown below, the action in a short story unfolds much more quickly than it does in most novels.

Short Story Structure
Meet **main characters** → Learn their **problems** → Sort out **complications**
→ Move to the story's **climax** → **Resolution**

Conflict is the struggle or battle that characters in a story face. In "Amigo Brothers," the two main characters face both external and internal conflicts. The two best friends must battle each other in a boxing ring, an external conflict. Each boy also struggles with this internal conflict, a conflict that happens inside a person's mind: How can he do his best in the ring and at the same time avoid hurting his best friend?

READING FOCUS: COMPARING AND CONTRASTING

You **compare** and **contrast** things all the time without even thinking about it. A comparison points out similarities between things; a contrast points out differences. When buying sneakers, for example, you may discover that although two pairs both are lace-up, nylon, and designed for running (points of comparison), you like the blue pair better than the white pair (point of contrast).

SKILLS FOCUS

Literary Skills
Understand a form of prose, the short story; understand internal and external conflict.

Reading Skills
Understand comparison and contrast.

Vocabulary Development

Amigo Brothers

SELECTION VOCABULARY

bouts (BOWTS) *n.:* matches; contests.
> *Both boxers had won many bouts.*

pensively (PEHN SIHV LEE) *adv.:* thoughtfully.
> *Felix nodded pensively as he rested.*

torrent (TAWR EHNT) *n.:* flood or rush.
> *A torrent of emotion left him close to tears.*

dispelled (DIH SPEHLD) *v.:* driven away.
> *All doubt was dispelled the moment Tony made up his mind.*

frenzied (FREHN ZEED) *adj.:* wild.
> *The audience's reaction was as frenzied as the battle in the ring.*

WORD STUDY

DIRECTIONS: Synonyms are words that have the same meaning. It's helpful when learning a new word to also learn its synonyms. Each sentence below contains an *italicized* word or phrase that is a synonym for one of the vocabulary words. Write the vocabulary word that matches each synonym on the blank following the sentence.

1. In a ninth-inning rally, the hitters poured out a *flood* of line drives on the tired infielders. _____

2. The champion boxer was undefeated in his last twenty *fights*.
_____

3. After winning the relay by six seconds, our swim team *drove away* our coach's fear that we couldn't work as a team. _____

4. A group of *wild* fans ran onto the field after the soccer final.
_____

5. Michelle studied the basket *thoughtfully* before the last-second free throw. _____

AMIGO BROTHERS

by Piri Thomas

BACKGROUND

This story is about two friends (*amigos* in Spanish) living on the Lower East Side of New York City. Many boys from the Lower East Side have dreamed of building a better life by winning the New York Golden Gloves, a boxing tournament started in 1927 by Paul Gallico, a newspaper writer. This tournament marks an amateur's entry into the world of big-time boxing.

A **LITERARY FOCUS**

Underline the names of the two **main characters**. Circle three details that tell how similar, or alike, they are. Why do you think the author wants us to know this?

_____

_____

_____

_____

_____

_____

_____

Antonio Cruz and Felix Vargas were both seventeen years old. They were so together in friendship that they felt themselves to be brothers. They had known each other since childhood, growing up on the Lower East Side of Manhattan in the same tenement[1] building on Fifth Street between Avenue A and Avenue B.

Antonio was fair, lean, and lanky, while Felix was dark, short, and husky. Antonio's hair was always falling over his eyes, while Felix wore his black hair in a natural Afro style.

10 Each youngster had a dream of someday becoming lightweight champion of the world. Every chance they had, the boys worked out, sometimes at the Boys' Club on 10th Street and Avenue A and sometimes at the pro's gym on 14th Street. Early morning sunrises would find them running along the East River Drive, wrapped in sweat shirts, short towels around their necks, and handkerchiefs Apache style around their foreheads. **A**

While some youngsters were into street negatives, Antonio and Felix slept, ate, rapped, and dreamt positive. Between them, they had a collection of *Fight* magazines second to none, plus

---

1. **tenement** *n.* used as *adj.:* apartment. Tenement buildings are often cheaply built and poorly maintained.

---

a scrapbook filled with torn tickets to every boxing match they
had ever attended, and some clippings of their own. If asked a
question about any given fighter, they would immediately zip out
from their memory banks divisions, weights, records of fights,
knockouts, technical knockouts, and draws or losses.

Each had fought many bouts representing their community and had won two gold-plated medals plus a silver and
bronze medallion. **B** The difference was in their style. Antonio's
lean form and long reach made him the better boxer, while
Felix's short and muscular frame made him the better slugger.
Whenever they had met in the ring for sparring sessions,[2] it had
always been hot and heavy. **C**

Now, after a series of elimination bouts, they had been
informed that they were to meet each other in the division finals
that were scheduled for the seventh of August, two weeks away—
the winner to represent the Boys' Club in the Golden Gloves
Championship Tournament. **D**

The two boys continued to run together along the East
River Drive. But even when joking with each other, they both
sensed a wall rising between them.

© Scott B. Rosen/Bill Smith Studio

2. **sparring sessions:** practice matches in which boxers use light punches.

B VOCABULARY

Selection Vocabulary

In boxing, a competition
between two boxers is called
a *bout*, just as a competition
between two baseball teams
is called a *game*. Why do
you think different terms are
used to label competitions in
different sports?

_____

_____

_____

_____

_____

C READING FOCUS

Underline the details in this
paragraph that describe each
youngster's fighting style.
How does the author **contrast** the two boxers' styles?

_____

_____

_____

_____

_____

_____

D READ AND DISCUSS

Comprehension

Knowing what you do about
Felix and Antonio, what do
you think they might feel
about having the opportu-
nity to fight in the Golden
Gloves Championship
Tournament?

Word Study

What might the word *ace-boon* mean here? Use context clues to help you.

_____

_____

_____

_____

_____

40 One morning less than a week before their bout, they met as usual for their daily workout. They fooled around with a few jabs at the air, slapped skin, and then took off, running lightly along the dirty East River's edge.

Antonio glanced at Felix, who kept his eyes purposely straight ahead, pausing from time to time to do some fancy leg work while throwing one-twos followed by uppercuts to an imaginary jaw. Antonio then beat the air with a barrage of body blows and short devastating lefts with an overhead jaw-breaking right.

After a mile or so, Felix puffed and said, "Let's stop a while, bro. I think we both got something to say to each other."

50 Antonio nodded. It was not natural to be acting as though nothing unusual was happening when two ace-boon buddies were going to be blasting each other within a few short days. **A**

They rested their elbows on the railing separating them from the river. Antonio wiped his face with his short towel. The sunrise was now creating day.

Felix leaned heavily on the river's railing and stared across to the shores of Brooklyn. Finally, he broke the silence.

"Man. I don't know how to come out with it."

Antonio helped. "It's about our fight, right?"

60 "Yeah, right." Felix's eyes squinted at the rising orange sun.

"I've been thinking about it too, panin.[3] In fact, since we found out it was going to be me and you, I've been awake at night, pulling punches on you, trying not to hurt you."

"Same here. It ain't natural not to think about the fight. I mean, we both are cheverote[4] fighters and we both want to win. But only one of us can win. There ain't no draws in the eliminations." **B**

Felix tapped Antonio gently on the shoulder. "I don't mean to sound like I'm bragging, bro. But I wanna win, fair and 70 square."

---

3. **panin** (PAH NEEN) *n.*: Puerto Rican Spanish slang for "pal" or "buddy."

4. **cheverote** (CHEH VEH RO TEH) *adj.*: Puerto Rican Spanish slang for "the greatest."

Antonio nodded quietly. "Yeah. We both know that in the ring the better man wins. Friend or no friend, brother or no …"

Felix finished it for him. "Brother. Tony, let's promise something right here. OK?"

"If it's fair, hermano,[5] I'm for it." Antonio admired the courage of a tugboat pulling a barge five times its welter-weight size.

"It's fair, Tony. When we get into the ring, it's gotta be like we never met. We gotta be like two heavy strangers that want the same thing and only one can have it. You understand, don't cha?"

80   "Sí, I know." Tony smiled. "No pulling punches. We go all the way."

"Yeah, that's right. Listen, Tony. Don't you think it's a good idea if we don't see each other until the day of the fight? I'm going to stay with my Aunt Lucy in the Bronx. I can use Gleason's Gym for working out. My manager says he got some sparring partners with more or less your style." **C**

Tony scratched his nose pensively. "Yeah, it would be better for our heads." He held out his hand, palm upward. "Deal?"

"Deal." Felix lightly slapped open skin. **D**

90   "Ready for some more running?" Tony asked lamely. **E**

"Naw, bro. Let's cut it here. You go on. I kinda like to get things together in my head."

"You ain't worried, are you?" Tony asked.

"No way, man." Felix laughed out loud. "I got too much smarts for that. I just think it's cooler if we split right here. After the fight, we can get it together again like nothing ever happened."

The amigo brothers were not ashamed to hug each other tightly.

100   "Guess you're right. Watch yourself, Felix. I hear there's some pretty heavy dudes up in the Bronx. Suavecito,[6] OK?"

"OK. You watch yourself too, sabe?"[7]

---

5. **hermano:** (EHR MAH NOH) *n.:* Spanish for "brother."

6. **suavecito** (SWAH VEH SEE TOH) *adj.:* Puerto Rican Spanish slang for "cool."

7. **sabe** (SAH BEH) *v.:* Spanish for "you know."

C VOCABULARY

Academic Vocabulary

In this paragraph, Felix tells Antonio that he plans to train alone. What *impact*, or effect, do you think this will have on their friendship?

_____

_____

_____

_____

D READ AND DISCUSS

What is happening between the boys here?

E LANGUAGE COACH

The suffix –*ly* usually turns adjectives into adverbs. Rewrite this sentence using the adjective *lame* rather than the adverb *lamely*.

_____

_____

Tony jogged away. Felix watched his friend disappear from view, throwing rights and lefts. Both fighters had a lot of psyching up to do before the big fight. A

The days in training passed much too slowly. Although they kept out of each other's way, they were aware of each other's progress via the ghetto grapevine.

The evening before the big fight, Tony made his way to the 110 roof of his tenement. In the quiet early dark, he peered over the ledge. Six stories below, the lights of the city blinked and the sounds of cars mingled with the curses and the laughter of children in the street. He tried not to think of Felix, feeling he had succeeded in psyching his mind. But only in the ring would he really know. To spare Felix hurt, he would have to knock him out, early and quick.

Up in the South Bronx, Felix decided to take in a movie in an effort to keep Antonio's face away from his fists. The flick was *The Champion* with Kirk Douglas, the third time Felix was 120 seeing it.

The champion was getting beaten, his face being pounded into raw, wet hamburger. His eyes were cut, jagged, bleeding, one eye swollen, the other almost shut. He was saved only by the sound of the bell.

Felix became the champ and Tony the challenger.

The movie audience was going out of its head, roaring in blood lust at the butchery going on. The champ hunched his shoulders, grunting and sniffing red blood back into his broken nose. The challenger, confident that he had the championship in 130 the bag, threw a left. The champ countered with a dynamite right that exploded into the challenger's brains.

Felix's right arm felt the shock. Antonio's face, superimposed on the screen, was shattered and split apart by the awesome force of the killer blow. Felix saw himself in the ring, blasting Antonio against the ropes. The champ had to be forcibly restrained. The challenger was allowed to crumble slowly to the canvas, a broken bloody mess.

When Felix finally left the theater, he had figured out how
to psych himself for tomorrow's fight. It was Felix the Champion
140   vs. Antonio the Challenger. **B**

He walked up some dark streets, deserted except for small
pockets of wary-looking kids wearing gang colors. Despite the
fact that he was Puerto Rican like them, they eyed him as a
stranger to their turf. Felix did a fast shuffle, bobbing and
weaving, while letting loose a torrent of blows that would
demolish whatever got in its way. **C** It seemed to impress the
brothers, who went about their own business.

Finding no takers, Felix decided to split to his aunt's.
Walking the streets had not relaxed him; neither had the fight
150   flick. All it had done was to stir him up. He let himself quietly
into his Aunt Lucy's apartment and went straight to bed, falling
into a fitful sleep with sounds of the gong for Round One.

Antonio was passing some heavy time on his rooftop. How
would the fight tomorrow affect his relationship with Felix? After
all, fighting was like any other profession. Friendship had nothing
to do with it. A gnawing doubt crept in. He cut negative thinking
real quick by doing some speedy fancy dance steps, bobbing and
weaving like mercury. The night air was blurred with perpetual
motions of left hooks and right crosses. Felix, his amigo brother,
160   was not going to be Felix at all in the ring. Just an opponent with
another face. Antonio went to sleep, hearing the opening bell for
the first round. Like his friend in the South Bronx, he prayed for
victory via a quick clean knockout in the first round. **D**

Large posters plastered all over the walls of local shops
announced the fight between Antonio Cruz and Felix Vargas as
the main bout.

The fight had created great interest in the neighborhood.
Antonio and Felix were well liked and respected. Each had his
own loyal following. Betting fever was high and ranged from a
170   bottle of Coke to cold hard cash on the line.

Antonio's fans bet with unbridled faith in his boxing skills.
On the other side, Felix's admirers bet on his dynamite-packed
fists.

B LITERARY FOCUS

How does Felix deal with his
internal **conflict** by watching
the movie?

_____
_____
_____
_____
_____

C VOCABULARY

Selection Vocabulary
The word _torrent_ means
"flood" or "rush." Why does
Felix release a torrent of
punches here?

_____
_____
_____
_____
_____

D READ AND DISCUSS

Comprehension
What is going on with the
boys now?

Felix had returned to his apartment early in the morning of August 7th and stayed there, hoping to avoid seeing Antonio. He turned the radio on to salsa[8] music sounds and then tried to read while waiting for word from his manager. **A**

The fight was scheduled to take place in Tompkins Square Park. It had been decided that the gymnasium of the Boys' Club
180 was not large enough to hold all the people who were sure to attend. In Tompkins Square Park, everyone who wanted could view the fight, whether from ringside or window fire escapes or tenement rooftops.

The morning of the fight Tompkins Square was a beehive of activity with numerous workers setting up the ring, the seats, and the guest speakers' stand. The scheduled bouts began shortly after noon and the park had begun filling up even earlier.

The local junior high school across from Tompkins Square Park served as the dressing room for all the fighters. Each was
190 given a separate classroom with desk tops, covered with mats, serving as resting tables. Antonio thought he caught a glimpse of Felix waving to him from a room at the far end of the corridor. He waved back just in case it had been him.

The fighters changed from their street clothes into fighting gear. Antonio wore white trunks, black socks, and black shoes. Felix wore sky-blue trunks, red socks, and white boxing shoes. They had dressing gowns to match their fighting trunks with their names neatly stitched on the back.

The loudspeakers blared into the open windows of the
200 school. There were speeches by dignitaries, community leaders, and great boxers of yesteryear. **B** Some were well prepared; some improvised on the spot. They all carried the same message of great pleasure and honor at being part of such a historic event. This great day was in the tradition of champions emerging from the streets of the Lower East Side. **C**

Interwoven with the speeches were the sounds of the other boxing events. After the sixth bout, Felix was much relieved

---

8. **salsa** (SAHL SAH) _n._ used as _adj._: Latin American dance music, usually played at fast tempos.

© SuperStock/Alamy

D **READING FOCUS**

Compare Felix's and Antonio's actions as they enter the ring and greet each other.

_____

_____

_____

_____

_____

_____

_____

when his trainer, Charlie, said, "Time change. Quick knockout. This is it. We're on."

210   Waiting time was over. Felix was escorted from the class-room by a dozen fans in white T-shirts with the word FELIX across their fronts.

Antonio was escorted down a different stairwell and guided through a roped-off path.

As the two climbed into the ring, the crowd exploded with a roar. Antonio and Felix both bowed gracefully and then raised their arms in acknowledgment.

Antonio tried to be cool, but even as the roar was in its first birth, he turned slowly to meet Felix's eyes looking directly into

220   his. Felix nodded his head and Antonio responded. And both as one, just as quickly, turned away to face his own corner. **D**

Bong—bong—bong. The roar turned to stillness.

"Ladies and Gentlemen, Señores y Señoras."

The announcer spoke slowly, pleased at his bilingual efforts.

"Now the moment we have all been waiting for—the main event between two fine young Puerto Rican fighters, products of our Lower East Side."

"Loisaida,"9 called out a member of the audience.

_____

9. **Loisaida** (LO EE SY DAH) *n*.: Puerto Rican English dialect for "Lower East Side."

A **READ AND DISCUSS**

How has the **conflict**
between the two friends
changed?

_____

_____

_____

_____

_____

_____

_____

"In this corner, weighing 134 pounds, Felix Vargas. And in this corner, weighing 133 pounds, Antonio Cruz. The winner will represent the Boys' Club in the tournament of champions, the Golden Gloves. There will be no draw. May the best man win." **A**

The cheering of the crowd shook the window panes of the old buildings surrounding Tompkins Square Park. At the center of the ring, the referee was giving instructions to the youngsters.

"Keep your punches up. No low blows. No punching on the back of the head. Keep your heads up. Understand? Let's have a clean fight. Now shake hands and come out fighting."

Both youngsters touched gloves and nodded. They turned and danced quickly to their corners. Their head towels and dressing gowns were lifted neatly from their shoulders by their trainers' nimble fingers. Antonio crossed himself. Felix did the same.

BONG! BONG! ROUND ONE. Felix and Antonio turned and faced each other squarely in a fighting pose. Felix wasted no time. He came in fast, head low, half-hunched toward his right shoulder, and lashed out with a straight left. He missed a right cross as Antonio slipped the punch and countered with one-two-three lefts that snapped Felix's head back, sending a mild shock coursing through him. If Felix had any small doubt about their friendship affecting their fight, it was being neatly dispelled.

Antonio danced, a joy to behold. His left hand was like a piston pumping jabs one right after another with seeming ease. Felix bobbed and weaved and never stopped boring in. He knew that at long range he was at a disadvantage. Antonio had too much reach on him. Only by coming in close could Felix hope to achieve the dreamed-of knockout.

Antonio knew the dynamite that was stored in his amigo brother's fist. He ducked a short right and missed a left hook. Felix trapped him against the ropes just long enough to pour some punishing rights and lefts to Antonio's hard midsection. Antonio slipped away from Felix, crashing two lefts to his head, which set Felix's right ear to ringing.

Bong! Both amigos froze a punch well on its way, sending up a roar of approval for good sportsmanship.

Felix walked briskly back to his corner. His right ear had not stopped ringing. Antonio gracefully danced his way toward his stool none the worse, except for glowing glove burns showing
270 angry red against the whiteness of his midribs. **B**

"Watch that right, Tony." His trainer talked into his ear. "Remember Felix always goes to the body. He'll want you to drop your hands for his overhand left or right. Got it?"

Antonio nodded, spraying water out between his teeth. He felt better as his sore midsection was being firmly rubbed.

Felix's corner was also busy.

"You gotta get in there, fella." Felix's trainer poured water over his curly Afro locks. "Get in there or he's gonna chop you up from way back." **C**

280 *Bong! Bong!* Round two. Felix was off his stool and rushed Antonio like a bull, sending a hard right to his head. Beads of water exploded from Antonio's long hair.

Antonio, hurt, sent back a blurring barrage of lefts and rights that only meant pain to Felix, who returned with a short left to the head followed by a looping right to the body. Antonio countered with his own flurry, forcing Felix to give ground. But not for long.

Felix bobbed and weaved, bobbed and weaved, occasionally punching his two gloves together.

290 Antonio waited for the rush that was sure to come. Felix closed in and feinted with his left shoulder and threw a right instead. Lights suddenly exploded inside Felix's head as Antonio slipped the blow and hit him with a pistonlike left, catching him flush on the point of his chin.

Bedlam broke loose as Felix's legs momentarily buckled. He fought off a series of rights and lefts and came back with a strong right that taught Antonio respect.

Antonio danced in carefully. He knew Felix had the habit of playing possum when hurt, to sucker an opponent within reach
300 of the powerful bombs he carried in each fist. **D**

B READING FOCUS

Compare and **contrast** the boys' actions. In lines 239–271 underline Antonio's actions. Circle Felix's actions. How are they similar and different?

_____

_____

_____

_____

C READ AND DISCUSS

Comprehension

What do you learn from the advice of the two trainers?

D VOCABULARY

Word Study

The author states that Felix had the habit of "playing possum when hurt". Possums (short for opossums) are animals that pretend to be asleep, ill, or dead when in danger. Why might Felix choose to "play possum" when boxing?

_____

_____

_____

_____

_____

_____

Selection Vocabulary

Frenzied means "wild." Why do you think the use of this word is appropriate in this scene?

_____

_____

_____

_____

_____

A right to the head slowed Antonio's pretty dancing. He answered with his own left at Felix's right eye that began puffing up within three seconds.

Antonio, a bit too eager, moved in too close, and Felix had him entangled into a rip-roaring, punching toe-to-toe slugfest that brought the whole Tompkins Square Park screaming to its feet.

Rights to the body. Lefts to the head. Neither fighter was giving an inch. Suddenly a short right caught Antonio squarely on the chin. His long legs turned to jelly and his arms flailed out desperately. Felix, grunting like a bull, threw wild punches from every direction. Antonio, groggy, bobbed and weaved, evading most of the blows. Suddenly his head cleared. His left flashed out hard and straight, catching Felix on the bridge of his nose.

Felix lashed back with a haymaker, right off the ghetto streets. At the same instant, his eye caught another left hook from Antonio. Felix swung out, trying to clear the pain. Only the frenzied screaming of those along ringside let him know that he had dropped Antonio. **A** Fighting off the growing haze, Antonio struggled to his feet, got up, ducked, and threw a smashing right that dropped Felix flat on his back.

Felix got up as fast as he could in his own corner, groggy but still game. He didn't even hear the count. In a fog, he heard the roaring of the crowd, who seemed to have gone insane. His head cleared to hear the bell sound at the end of the round. He was glad. His trainer sat him down on the stool. **B**

In his corner, Antonio was doing what all fighters do when they are hurt. They sit and smile at everyone.

The referee signaled the ring doctor to check the fighters out. He did so and then gave his OK. The cold-water sponges brought clarity to both amigo brothers. They were rubbed until their circulation ran free.

Bong! Round three—the final round. Up to now it had been tic-tac-toe, pretty much even. But everyone knew there could be no draw and that this round would decide the winner.

© Scott B. Rosen/Bill Smith Studio

C READ AND DISCUSS

Comprehension

How does round three connect to the boys' fears of fighting their best fights?

This time, to Felix's surprise, it was Antonio who came out fast, charging across the ring. Felix braced himself but couldn't ward off the barrage of punches. Antonio drove Felix hard against the ropes.

340   The crowd ate it up. Thus far the two had fought with mucho corazón.[10] Felix tapped his gloves and commenced his attack anew. Antonio, throwing boxer's caution to the winds, jumped in to meet him.

Both pounded away. Neither gave an inch and neither fell to the canvas. Felix's left eye was tightly closed. Claret-red blood poured from Antonio's nose. They fought toe-to-toe.

The sounds of their blows were loud in contrast to the silence of a crowd gone completely mute. The referee was stunned by their savagery.

350   *Bong! Bong! Bong!* The bell sounded over and over again. Felix and Antonio were past hearing. Their blows continued to pound on each other like hailstones.

Finally the referee and the two trainers pried Felix and Antonio apart. Cold water was poured over them to bring them back to their senses. **C**

They looked around and then rushed toward each other. A cry of alarm surged through Tompkins Square Park. Was this a fight to the death instead of a boxing match?

---

10. **mucho corazón** (MOO CHO KO RA SOHN): Spanish for "a lot of heart."

The fear soon gave way to wave upon wave of cheering as the two amigos embraced.

No matter what the decision, they knew they would always be champions to each other.

BONG! BONG! BONG! "Ladies and Gentlemen. Señores and Señoras. The winner and representative to the Golden Gloves Tournament of Champions is …"

The announcer turned to point to the winner and found himself alone. Arm in arm the champions had already left the ring. A

Applying Your Skills

Amigo Brothers

VOCABULARY DEVELOPMENT

DIRECTIONS: Write vocabulary words from the Word Box on the correct blanks to complete the paragraph. Not all words will be used.

Word Box

- bouts
- pensively
- torrent
- dispelled
- frenzied

Antonio landed a hard jab. Any doubts that Felix had about the seriousness of this fight were (1) _____. Out of all of the (2) _____ they had fought, this was the hardest one for both boys. Thinking of their friendship, Antonio was overcome by a (3) _____ of memories and emotions. Felix returned a blow, which drew applause from the (4) _____ fans.

LITERARY FOCUS: THE SHORT STORY

DIRECTIONS: Review the elements of the short story introduced in the Preparing to Read section. Then, answer the questions below.

1. Provide an example of a **conflict** that arises during the story.

_____

2. The part of the story where Felix and Antonio hug and walk out of the ring before the winner is announced is considered the

   a) conflict.

   b) resolution.

   c) climax.

   d) complication.

READING FOCUS: COMPARING AND CONTRASTING

DIRECTIONS: Review the boys' friendship at the beginning and the ending of the story. On a separate piece of paper, write a short paragraph in which you **compare** and **contrast** their friendship before and after their bout. Remember that comparisons deal with similarities and that contrasts deal with differences.

SKILLS FOCUS

Literary Skills
Review the elements of the short story.

Reading Skills
Compare and contrast elements of the story.

Empress Theodora
by The World Almanac

INFORMATIONAL TEXT FOCUS: NOTE TAKING

Note taking helps you organize the facts you encounter as you read. You can also look over your notes later to help you recall what you have read. In order to take good notes, you should:

- **Find the main ideas.** The **main ideas** are the most important points in an article. You can often find these important ideas described in subheadings and in the first and last sentences of each paragraph.

- **Be organized.** List each main idea and its supporting details in the order that they appear.

- **Be brief.** Write only the most important words and phrases.

- **Underline or circle information.** If you own the book or article it may be useful to highlight key points.

SELECTION VOCABULARY

profession (PRUH FEH SHUHN) *n.:* paid occupation.
> *Acting was not seen as a respectable profession in the Byzantine Empire.*

forbade (FAWR BAYD) *v.:* ordered not to; outlawed.
> *A Byzantine law once forbade high-ranking men from marrying women of lower classes.*

facilitate (FUH SIHL UH TAYT) *v.:* ease; aid.
> *Theodora's influence helped facilitate changes to Byzantine society.*

WORD STUDY

DIRECTIONS: Writers will often restate a difficult term using simpler words. This helps make the meaning of the term clearer to the reader. The meaning of a term often appears close to that term in the text. In the passage below, look for the meaning of the word *facilitate* and underline it.

Theodora and Justinian built new bridges to *facilitate* transportation in Byzantium. These bridges made it easier for people and goods to move throughout the city.

SKILLS FOCUS

Informational Text Skills
Learn how to take notes.

EMPRESS THEODORA

by The World Almanac

> ### BACKGROUND
> When the Roman Empire split in two, the eastern half became known as the Byzantine Empire. Justinian I became one of the greatest Byzantine emperors. At his side was one of the most influential women of her time, the Empress Theodora.

The Court of Theodora, Detail: Bust of Theodora and courtesan.
© S. Vitale, Ravenna, Italy. Scala/Art Resource, New York.

A VOCABULARY

Word Study

In this sentence, the poverty of Theodora's family is contrasted with her high rank later in life. You can conclude that in this case *humble* means "of low status or rank." What is another meaning of *humble*?

_____

_____

_____

At a time when women had little or no political power, Theodora, empress of the Byzantine Empire, was a rare exception. Though from poor and humble beginnings, she helped maintain her husband's empire as Persian forces threatened from the east and Germanic invaders continued attacking from the west. **A** Born about A.D. 500, she was the daughter of a

The word *profession* comes from the Latin **word root** *professio*, which means "to declare publicly." How are the words *professor* and *professional* related to *profession*?

_____

_____

_____

_____

C **READING FOCUS**

When you are **note taking**, keep an eye out for the **main ideas**. This subhead introduces a main idea about Theodora's accomplishments. Write the main idea below.

_____

_____

_____

bear keeper who worked in Constantinople's Hippodrome, a stadium in which horse races and often violent, bloody perfor-mances were held. Her father died when she was young, forcing Theodora and her sister to support themselves. They became actors, which at the time was considered a low-class profession, especially for women. **A**

At the age of sixteen, Theodora traveled widely, performing throughout North Africa and the Middle East. Six years later she stopped acting, returned to Constantinople, and became a wool spinner. The beautiful and witty young woman met Justinian, the heir to the throne of his uncle, Justin I. Justinian, the future lead-er of the Byzantine Empire, and Theodora fell in love andwanted to marry. However, a long-standing law forbade high-ranking men from marrying women of lower classes. **B**

Influencing Legal and Social Reform **C**

From the beginning of their relationship, Theodora promoted freedom and equality for women. She had Justinian ask his uncle to repeal the law that kept the couple from marrying. Justin I agreed, and at age twenty-five, Theodora married Justinian.

Soon after their marriage, Justinian became emperor. Although Theodora was not officially a joint ruler, Justinian treated her as his intellectual equal and sought her opinions and input on many of his important decisions.

Raising the Status of Women

Under Empress Theodora's influence, Justinian began to examine the empire's laws carefully. Many of these changes were aimed at protecting women and children. Justinian passed laws that raised the status of women higher than it had ever been in the empire. Divorced women were granted rights, such as the abil-ity to remain guardians of their children. He allowed women to own their own property. The custom of abandoning infants, most always girls, to die of exposure[1] was outlawed. Other laws established hospitals, orphanages, and care facilities for the needy. Justinian organized existing Roman laws, plus his new ones, into the Justinian Code, which has served as a model for the laws of many later nations.

Saving the Empire

Theodora used her intelligence and skill as a leader to save and strengthen the Byzantine Empire. In A.D. 532, as a chariot race was about to begin at the Hippodrome, political rivals there opposed to the emperor joined in a violent protest, now known as the Nika revolt. This riot quickly engulfed the city, and the rebels burned huge areas of Constantinople. Convinced of defeat, Justinian and his advisors prepared to flee the city in ships. With one of the greatest short speeches ever recorded, the empress persuaded them not to flee to the shame of safety, but to fight with courage to the death. His confidence bolstered, Justinian roused his generals and crushed the rebellion. Her speech probably saved the city, the empire—and Justinian's throne. **D**

Rebuilding the City

After the revolt, Theodora and Justinian worked together to rebuild and improve the ruined city. They added new aqueducts

D **READ AND DISCUSS**

Comprehension
How do Theodora's actions during the riot add to what you know about her?

© Gianna Dagil Orti/Corbis

---

1. **exposure** (EHK SPOH ZHUR) *n.:* physical condition resulting from being left open to danger without the protection of clothing or shelter, especially in severe weather.

A READING FOCUS

The concluding paragraph of an informational article often has a summary of the **main ideas** in the text. What key words and phrases from this summary would you include in your **note taking** for this article?

_____

_____

_____

_____

B READING FOCUS

Look for the **main ideas** in Theodora's speech. Why does she say Justinian should stay in the city? What does this speech suggest about her relationship with Justinian?

_____

_____

_____

_____

_____

_____

The Court of Theodora. © Archivo Iconografico, S.A./Corbis

to provide clean drinking water, bridges to facilitate transportation, and hostels[2] to shelter the homeless. They also built numerous churches, including the beautiful Hagia Sophia—one of the most famous buildings in the world—which still exists in
60   Istanbul as a museum.

Leaving a Legacy

Theodora, the daughter of a lowly bear keeper, rose to have a significant impact on the Byzantine Empire. As wife to Emperor Justinian I, her intelligence and courage made the empire a safer and fairer place. Laws that she initiated influenced legal systems that exist to this day. **A**

> "If, now, it is your wish to save yourself, O Emperor, there is no difficulty. For we have much money, and there is the sea, here the boats. However consider whether it will not come about after you have been saved that you would gladly exchange that
> 70   safety for death. For as for myself, I approve a certain ancient saying that royalty is a good burial-shroud." **B**
>
> – *Empress Theodora*

2.   **hostels** (HAH STUHLZ) *n.:* shelters for those without a home; supervised residences.

Applying Your Skills

Empress Theodora

VOCABULARY DEVELOPMENT

DIRECTIONS: Write vocabulary words from the Word Box on the correct blanks to complete the paragraph. Some words may be used more than once.

Word Box

facilitate

forbade

profession

As a young woman, Theodora and her sisters worked as actors, a
(1) _____ that was not respected by Byzantine society.
Later she joined a more well-regarded (2) _____ as a
wool spinner. At first, her marriage plans were blocked by a
law that (3) _____ men and women from different social
classes from marrying. To (4) _____ her marriage,
however, the law was changed. As Empress, Theodora was able to
(5) _____ more changes in Byzantine law that improved
the position of certain people in society.

INFORMATIONAL TEXT FOCUS: NOTE TAKING

DIRECTIONS: Use the **notes** you took to answer the following questions.

1. What was Theodora's social status early in life?

   _____

2. How was Theodora able to influence Byzantine law and society?

   _____

   _____

3. What changes to Byzantine society did Theodora help bring about?

   _____

   _____

4. How did Theodora help save the Byzantine Empire?

   _____

   _____

5. Why do you think Theodora was an important historical figure?

   _____

   _____

SKILLS FOCUS

Informational Text Skills
Learn how to take notes.

The Hippodrome
by The World Almanac

INFORMATIONAL TEXT READING FOCUS: SUMMARIZING AN INFORMATIONAL TEXT

A **summary** restates the **main ideas** of a text in a simpler and shorter form. A summary can help you remember important points you might otherwise forget. To write a good summary:

- Include the author and title of the article.

- State the topic of the article in a few words.

- Retell the events or main points of the article in your own words.

- Sum up the writer's main idea.

Read the text carefully to decide what details to leave in and what to leave out. If someone who has not read the article can understand its main points after reading your summary, you have done a good job.

Use the Skill After reading "The Hippodrome," write a summary describing the Hippodrome and its importance to the Byzantine people.

SELECTION VOCABULARY

renovation (REHN UH VAY SHUHN) *n.:* restoration of something to make it better.
> *The renovation made the Hippodrome better than it had been in years.*

spectators (SPEHK TAY TUHRZ) *n.:* people who watch an event.
> *The Hippodrome may have held as many as 100,000 spectators.*

barbarian (BAHR BAYR EE UHN) *adj.:* a member of a group felt to be uncivilized and inferior by another group.
> *Romans often considered barbarian tribes to be less advanced.*

WORD STUDY

DIRECTIONS: Writers often explain unfamiliar words in the surrounding text. By looking for words and phrases including *for example, like, such as,* and *as if,* you may find an explanation of an unfamiliar word. In the examples below, circle the text that explains the meaning of the vocabulary term.

1. The guests were *barbarians*. It was as if they had never seen silverware or had a civilized meal.

2. The stadium needs a major *renovation* before its condition improves.

SKILLS FOCUS

Informational Text Skills
Summarize a text.

THE HIPPODROME

by The World Almanac

> **BACKGROUND**
> The Romans had a tradition of building stadiums for public entertainment in their cities. Perhaps the most famous of these stadiums is the Coliseum in the city of Rome. The Hippodrome of Byzantium was even larger in size, attracting thousands of people for public events.

At the beginning of the third century A.D., Roman troops destroyed the eastern city of Byzantium, and the new emperor set to rebuilding it larger than before. To provide residents with entertainment that they were used to in Rome, he built the Hippodrome, the largest stadium in the ancient world. A hundred years later, another Roman emperor, Constantine, moved the empire's capital from Rome to Byzantium, renaming the city Constantinople after himself. One of his major building projects was the renovation of the Hippodrome. **A**

10   The Hippodrome was the center of Constantinople's social life. The Hippodrome's main function was as a horse- and chariot-racing track. (The term *hippodrome* comes from the Greek words *hippos* ("horse") and *dromos* ("path" or "way"). However, it also was the place to see royal ceremonies, parades of victorious generals, political demonstrations, and public executions. Acrobats, clowns, plays performed by actors, and fights between wild animals also entertained the crowds. **B**

The stadium's arena is estimated to have been almost 525 yards (about five football fields) long and 129 yards wide.
20   Some say it held as many as 100,000 spectators. Constantine decorated the center of the racetrack with monuments and statues, which could be tilted or removed so they wouldn't block the fans' view of the races. He and later emperors adorned the

A VOCABULARY

Selection Vocabulary
Look up the meaning of the word *renovation*. What does its use here tell you about the condition of the Hippodrome when Constantine arrived?

_____

_____

_____

_____

B READING FOCUS

This paragraph describes the many uses of the Hippodrome. **Summarize** these uses below.

_____

_____

_____

_____

B **READING FOCUS**

Summarize who the Blues and the Greens were and why they were important.

_____

_____

_____

_____

_____

_____

_____

_____

_____

C **READ AND DISCUSS**

Comprehension

How does the grand Hippodrome of the Byzantine Empire compare to the Hippodrome of today?

Hippodrome with artworks and religious items from all over the empire and the "barbarian" East. **A**

The races at the Hippodrome were extremely important to the heavy-betting citizens of Constantinople: Loyalty to certain racing teams divided them into groups so strong that they came to represent political differences as well. (Imagine Republicans

30 rooting for one basketball team, and Democrats for another.) In A.D. 532, supporters of two teams, the Blues and the Greens, came together to oppose Emperor Justinian I's policies. They began a protest in the Hippodrome that quickly turned into a violent riot, later known as the Nika revolt. **B** As flames engulfed much of the city, Emperor Justinian and his advisors were considering fleeing to safety. To stop them, Justinian's wife, Empress Theodora, delivered a powerful speech, declaring that she refused to give up her throne. This speech encouraged Justinian, and he sent troops to the Hippodrome to put down

40 the riot. Exits were blocked, and thirty to forty thousand protesters were killed in the stadium. Constantinople lay in ruins, but Justinian and Theodora remained in power.

Over the centuries, the Hippodrome declined in importance and beauty. Constantinople was sacked by Crusaders,[1] and in 1453, Ottoman Turks captured the city, changed its name to Istanbul, and used the stones of the Hippodrome as building material. Today, the ruins of the stadium are a public park with few monuments and artworks remaining. **C**

© Dorling Kindersley

---

1. Invading Crusaders looted the Hippodrome in 1204. Among the artwork they took were four famous bronze horses which were taken to Venice and are still there, above Saint Mark's Church.

Applying Your Skills

The Hippodrome

VOCABULARY DEVELOPMENT

DIRECTIONS: Read each sentence carefully. Then find and underline the definition of the boldfaced word within each sentence.

1. The city wall was undergoing **renovation**, as workers restored it to a better condition.

2. The Emperor thought the visitors were **barbarians** because they came from foreign lands and seemed uncivilized.

3. So many people came to watch the event that there were thousands of **spectators** in the stadium.

INFORMATIONAL TEXT FOCUS: SUMMARIZING AN INFORMATIONAL TEXT

DIRECTIONS: The first column of the chart below contains a **main idea** from "The Hippodrome." The second column provides a short **summary** of the facts that support this main idea. Fill in the blank boxes in the chart with the correct information. Then, on a separate sheet of paper, use the chart to help you write a summary of the entire article.

Main Idea	Summary of Details
The Hippodrome was important to the social life of Constantinople.	1.
2.	The Hippodrome was the length of five football fields and could hold as many as 100,000 people.
The Hippodrome was important in the politics of Constantinople.	3.
The Hippodrome was the scene of a key event in the history of the Byzantine Empire.	4.
5.	Constantinople was sacked by the Crusaders and later conquered by the Ottoman Turks.

SKILLS FOCUS

Informational Text Skills
Summarize the text.

Collection 1

VOCABULARY REVIEW

DIRECTIONS: Match each word below with the word or phrase that best explains its meaning.

_____ **1.** bouts		**a.** ordered not to
_____ **2.** barbarian		**b.** contests
_____ **3.** forbade		**c.** flood
_____ **4.** dispelled		**d.** paid occupation
_____ **5.** pensively		**e.** rebuilding
_____ **6.** profession		**f.** wild
_____ **7.** frenzied		**g.** watchers
_____ **8.** torrent		**h.** thoughtfully
_____ **9.** renovation		**i.** driven away
_____ **10.** spectators		**j.** uncivilized person

Word Box

barbarian

bouts

dispelled

facilitate

forbade

frenzied

impact

interpret

insight

pensively

profession

renovation

significance

spectators

torrent

DIRECTIONS: Write vocabulary words from the Word Box on the correct blanks to complete the paragraph. Not all of the words in the Word Box will be used, and no words will be used more than once.

Good historical records can provide great (11) _____ about the importance of people. Having all the facts about historical figures' words, thoughts, and actions can help us to determine their (12) _____ on the world around them. Even the most important people in history would have little or no (13) _____ to us today if there were no records about them. Imagine how we might (14) _____ the importance of Albert Einstein if all we knew about him was that he once dropped out of school! Yes, good information does (15) _____ the sometimes difficult understanding of how people affected history.

Collection 1

LANGUAGE COACH

DIRECTIONS: Many English words have their roots in the Latin language. A **word root** is a word or part of a word from which other words are made. The list below shows the roots of several vocabulary words from the reading selections. Write the vocabulary word from the Word Box that is made from each root provided below.

1. *renovare*, to make new: _____

2. *barbarus*, foreign: _____

3. *spectare*, to watch: _____

4. *facere*, to do: _____

ORAL LANGUAGE ACTIVITY

DIRECTIONS: Prepare a brief presentation summarizing either "Amigo Brothers," "Empress Theodora," or "The Hippodrome."

- Begin by taking notes on your topic. Remember to look for the main ideas in the text.

- Use your notes to help you write a short summary of your topic—no more than a few sentences—to use as an introduction.

- Your notes should include some interesting details that help explain the main points you have noted.

Plot and Setting

July Afternoon by Anne Belov © A. Belov/Corbis

Literary and Academic Vocabulary for Collection 2

accurate (AK YUHR IHT) *adj.:* free from mistakes.
A summary should include accurate information.

adequate (AD UH KWIHT) *adj.:* enough for what is needed.
A plot summary should include an adequate number of main events.

similar (SIHM UH LUHR) *adj.:* almost the same.
Sometimes characters in a story act in similar ways.

significant (SIHG NIHF UH KUHNT) *adj.:* important.
A plot summary should include only significant details.

plot (PLAHT) *n.:* a series of related events that grow out of each other to make a story.
The plot of a story can be simple or complex.

suspense (SUH SPEHNS) *n.:* a kind of anxious curiosity.
As the child opens the locked door, the reader is filled with suspense about what is behind it.

foreshadowing (FAWR SHAH DOH IHNG) *v.:* giving hints or clues about what will happen next in the plot.
Learning that a character is afraid of snakes could be foreshadowing that he or she will encounter a snake later in the story.

Rikki-tikki-tavi

by Rudyard Kipling

LITERARY FOCUS: CONFLICT

In just about every story you read, the characters struggle in some way to get what they want or need. This struggle is called **conflict**. A story's **plot** unfolds as the characters take steps to achieve a goal and resolve conflicts along the way. The chart below maps out the conflicts that a main character might face in a story about a girl who wants to run a marathon.

Main Character	Goal
Josie	Josie wants to win a marathon.
Conflicts Josie Faces and Plot Events That Result	
Josie's parents worry that her training will interfere with her schoolwork, so she shows them that she can keep up with it.	
Josie's training is not going well, so she persuades a running coach to work with her after school.	
Josie doesn't have the money to register for the race, so she sells T-shirts to raise funds.	
Conflict resolved: Josie wins the race.	

SKILLS FOCUS

Literary Skills
Understand conflict.

Reading Skills
Summarize a text.

READING FOCUS: SUMMARIZING

You probably practice **summarizing** in real life without knowing it—telling a friend about the events of an exciting movie or filling your neighbor in on a story you just read, for instance. When you summarize a story, you use your own words to restate the **main ideas**, or major events.

Use the Skill   As you read "Rikki-tikki-tavi," keep track of major events and practice summarizing them.

Vocabulary Development

Rikki-tikki-tavi

SELECTION VOCABULARY

immensely (IH MEHNS LEE) *adv.:* enormously.
> *Rikki is immensely brave.*

cowered (KOW UHRD) *v.:* crouched and trembled in fear.
> *Darzee cowered before the snakes.*

valiant (VAL YUHNT) *adv.:* brave and determined.
> *Rikki is a valiant hero.*

consolation (KON SUH LAY SHUN) *v.:* comfort.
> *Rikki's consolation comes from protecting the family.*

WORD STUDY

DIRECTIONS: Match each vocabulary word in the first column with its synonym in the second column. A synonym is a word with the same or nearly the same definition as another word.

_____ 1. immensely   a. relief

_____ 2. cowered   b. courageous

_____ 3. valiant   c. hugely

_____ 4. consolation   d. hid

RIKKI-TIKKI-TAVI

by Rudyard Kipling

BACKGROUND

This story takes place in India many years ago, at a time when the British were in control. The family in this story lives in a cantonment (KAN TAWN MUHNT), which is a kind of army base. The father is in the British army. This story is about a conflict between two deadly snakes and a brave little mongoose—a creature that looks something like a weasel or a large squirrel.

A READ AND DISCUSS

Comprehension
What has the author told you about Rikki-tikki so far?

_____
_____
_____
_____
_____
_____
_____
_____

This is the story of the great war that Rikki-tikki-tavi fought single-handed, through the bathrooms of the big bungalow[1] in Segowlee cantonment.[2] Darzee, the tailorbird, helped him, and Chuchundra, the muskrat, who never comes out into the middle of the floor but always creeps round by the wall, gave him advice; but Rikki-tikki did the real fighting.

He was a mongoose, rather like a little cat in his fur and his tail but quite like a weasel in his head and his habits. His eyes and the end of his restless nose were pink; he could scratch
10 himself anywhere he pleased with any leg, front or back, that he chose to use; he could fluff up his tail till it looked like a bottlebrush, and his war cry as he scuttled through the long grass was *Rikk-tikk-tikki-tikki-tchk!* **A**

One day, a high summer flood washed him out of the burrow where he lived with his father and mother and carried him, kicking and clucking, down a roadside ditch. He found a little wisp of grass floating there and clung to it till he lost his senses. When he revived, he was lying in the hot sun

---

1. **bungalow** (BUHN GUH LOH) *n.:* in India, a low, one-storied house, named after a type of house found in Bengal, a region of South Asia.
2. **Segowlee** (SEE GOW LEE) **cantonment**: British army post in Segowlee (now Segauli), India.

in the middle of a garden path, very draggled[3] indeed, and a small boy was saying: "Here's a dead mongoose. Let's have a funeral."

"No," said his mother; "let's take him in and dry him. Perhaps he isn't really dead."

They took him into the house, and a big man picked him up between his finger and thumb and said he was not dead but half choked; so they wrapped him in cotton wool and warmed him over a little fire, and he opened his eyes and sneezed.

"Now," said the big man (he was an Englishman who had just moved into the bungalow), "don't frighten him, and we'll see what he'll do." **B**

It is the hardest thing in the world to frighten a mongoose, because he is eaten up from nose to tail with curiosity. The motto of all the mongoose family is "Run and find out," and Rikki-tikki was a true mongoose. He looked at the cotton wool, decided that it was not good to eat, ran all round the table, sat up and put his fur in order, scratched himself, and jumped on the small boy's shoulder.

"Don't be frightened, Teddy," said his father. "That's his way of making friends."

"Ouch! He's tickling under my chin," said Teddy.

Rikki-tikki looked down between the boy's collar and neck, snuffed at his ear, and climbed down to the floor, where he sat rubbing his nose.

"Good gracious," said Teddy's mother, "and that's a wild creature! I suppose he's so tame because we've been kind to him." **C**

"All mongooses are like that," said her husband. "If Teddy doesn't pick him up by the tail or try to put him in a cage, he'll run in and out of the house all day long. Let's give him something to eat."

They gave him a little piece of raw meat. Rikki-tikki liked it immensely, and when it was finished, he went out into the

---

3. **draggled** *v.* used as *adj.*: wet and muddy, as if from being dragged around.

B READING FOCUS

Summarize how Rikki gets to the bungalow.

_____
_____
_____
_____
_____
_____

C VOCABULARY

Academic Vocabulary

How is Rikki-tikki *similar* to average American house pets? How is he different?

_____
_____
_____
_____
_____
_____

Selection Vocabulary

The adjective *immense* means "huge" or "vast." Knowing this, what do you think the adverb *immensely* means in this sentence?

_____

_____

_____

B **READ AND DISCUSS**

Comprehension

How are things looking for Rikki-tikki? What does he think of his new family?

C **READ AND DISCUSS**

Comprehension

What have you learned about the relationship between Rikki-tikki and his new family?

veranda[4] and sat in the sunshine and fluffed up his fur to make it dry to the roots. A Then he felt better.

"There are more things to find out about in this house," he said to himself, "than all my family could find out in all their lives. I shall certainly stay and find out." B

He spent all that day roaming over the house. He nearly drowned himself in the bathtubs, put his nose into the ink on a writing table, and burnt it on the end of the big man's cigar, for he climbed up in the big man's lap to see how writing was done. At nightfall he ran into Teddy's nursery to watch how kerosene lamps were lighted, and when Teddy went to bed, Rikki-tikki climbed up too; but he was a restless companion, because he had to get up and attend to every noise all through the night and find out what made it. Teddy's mother and father came in, the last thing, to look at their boy, and Rikki-tikki was awake on the pillow. "I don't like that," said Teddy's mother; "he may bite the child." "He'll do no such thing," said the father. "Teddy's safer with that little beast than if he had a bloodhound to watch him. If a snake came into the nursery now—"

But Teddy's mother wouldn't think of anything so awful.

Early in the morning, Rikki-tikki came to early breakfast in the veranda riding on Teddy's shoulder, and they gave him banana and some boiled egg; and he sat on all their laps one after the other, because every well-brought-up mongoose always hopes to be a house mongoose someday and have rooms to run about in; and Rikki-tikki's mother (she used to live in the General's house at Segowlee) had carefully told Rikki what to do if ever he came across white men. C

Then Rikki-tikki went out into the garden to see what was to be seen. It was a large garden, only half cultivated, with bushes, as big as summerhouses, of Marshal Niel roses; lime and orange trees; clumps of bamboos; and thickets of high grass. Rikki-tikki licked his lips. "This is a splendid hunting ground," he said, and his tail grew bottlebrushy at the thought of it, and

---

4. **veranda** (VUH RAN DUH) *n.:* open porch covered by a roof, running along the outside of a building.

© Dinodia/Omni-Photo Communications

he scuttled up and down the garden, snuffing here and there till he heard very sorrowful voices in a thorn bush. It was Darzee, the tailorbird, and his wife. They had made a beautiful nest by pulling two big leaves together and stitching them up the edges

90 with fibers and had filled the hollow with cotton and downy fluff. The nest swayed to and fro as they sat on the rim and cried. **D**

"What is the matter?" asked Rikki-tikki.

"We are very miserable," said Darzee. "One of our babies fell out of the nest yesterday and Nag ate him."

"H'm!" said Rikki-tikki, "that is very sad—but I am a stranger here. Who is Nag?"

Darzee and his wife only cowered down in the nest without answering, for from the thick grass at the foot of the

100 bush there came a low hiss—a horrid, cold sound that made Rikki-tikki jump back two clear feet. **E** Then inch by inch out of the grass rose up the head and spread hood of Nag, the big black cobra, and he was five feet long from tongue to tail. When he had lifted one third of himself clear of the ground, he stayed balancing to and fro exactly as a dandelion tuft balances in the wind, and he looked at Rikki-tikki with the wicked snake's eyes

D LITERARY FOCUS

You will soon find out about Darzee's **conflict**. What do you think that conflict might be?

_____

_____

_____

E VOCABULARY

Selection Vocabulary

Darzee and his wife are afraid of Nag. Considering this, guess the definition of the word _cowered_ in this sentence.

_____

_____

_____

_____

Do you think a **conflict**, will develop between Rikki and Nag? Why or why not?

_____

_____

_____

_____

_____

_____

_____

that never change their expression, whatever the snake may be thinking of.

"Who is Nag," said he. "*I am* Nag. The great God Brahm[5] 110 put his mark upon all our people, when the first cobra spread his hood to keep the sun off Brahm as he slept. Look, and be afraid!"

He spread out his hood more than ever, and Rikki-tikki saw the spectacle mark on the back of it that looks exactly like the eye part of a hook-and-eye fastening. He was afraid for the minute; but it is impossible for a mongoose to stay frightened for any length of time, and though Rikki-tikki had never met a live cobra before, his mother had fed him on dead ones, and he knew that all a grown mongoose's business in life was to fight 120 and eat snakes. Nag knew that too, and at the bottom of his cold heart, he was afraid. **A**

"Well," said Rikki-tikki, and his tail began to fluff up again, "marks or no marks, do you think it is right for you to eat fledglings out of a nest?"

Nag was thinking to himself and watching the least little movement in the grass behind Rikki-tikki. He knew that mongooses in the garden meant death sooner or later for him and his family, but he wanted to get Rikki-tikki off his guard. So he dropped his head a little and put it on one side.

130 "Let us talk," he said. "You eat eggs. Why should not I eat birds?"

"Behind you! Look behind you!" sang Darzee.

Rikki-tikki knew better than to waste time in staring. He jumped up in the air as high as he could go, and just under him whizzed by the head of Nagaina, Nag's wicked wife. She had crept up behind him as he was talking, to make an end of him; and he heard her savage hiss as the stroke missed. He came down almost across her back, and if he had been an old mongoose, he would have known that then was the time to 140 break her back with one bite; but he was afraid of the terrible

---

5. **Brahm** (BRAHM): in the Hindu religion, the creator (also called Brahma).

lashing return stroke of the cobra. He bit, indeed, but did not
bite long enough, and he jumped clear of the whisking tail,
leaving Nagaina torn and angry.

"Wicked, wicked Darzee!" said Nag, lashing up as high
as he could reach toward the nest in the thorn bush; but
Darzee had built it out of reach of snakes, and it only swayed
to and fro.

Rikki-tikki felt his eyes growing red and hot (when a
mongoose's eyes grow red, he is angry), and he sat back on
150   his tail and hind legs like a little kangaroo, and looked all
round him, and chattered with rage. But Nag and Nagaina had
disappeared into the grass. When a snake misses its stroke, it
never says anything or gives any sign of what it means to do
next. Rikki-tikki did not care to follow them, for he did not feel
sure that he could manage two snakes at once. So he trotted
off to the gravel path near the house and sat down to think. It
was a serious matter for him. **B** If you read the old books of
natural history, you will find they say that when the mongoose
fights the snake and happens to get bitten, he runs off and eats
160   some herb that cures him. That is not true. The victory is only a
matter of quickness of eye and quickness of foot—snake's blow
against the mongoose's jump—and as no eye can follow the
motion of a snake's head when it strikes, this makes things much
more wonderful than any magic herb. Rikki-tikki knew he was a
young mongoose, and it made him all the more pleased to think
that he had managed to escape a blow from behind. It gave him
confidence in himself, and when Teddy came running down the
path, Rikki-tikki was ready to be petted. But just as Teddy was
stooping, something wriggled a little in the dust and a tiny voice
170   said: "Be careful. I am Death!" It was Karait, the dusty brown
snakeling that lies for choice on the dusty earth; and his bite is as
dangerous as the cobra's. But he is so small that nobody thinks
of him, and so he does the more harm to people. **C** **D**

Rikki-tikki's eyes grew red again, and he danced up to Karait
with the peculiar rocking, swaying motion that he had inherited
from his family. It looks very funny, but it is so perfectly balanced

B READING FOCUS

Summarize what happens
between Rikki-tikki and the
snakes.

_____
_____
_____
_____
_____
_____
_____

C READ AND DISCUSS

Comprehension
What does Rikki-tikki-tavi
learn from his encounter
with Nagaina?

D LITERARY FOCUS

Do you think a **conflict** will
develop between Rikki-tikki
and Karait? Why or why not?

_____
_____
_____
_____

© Mira/Alamy

a gait[6] that you can fly off from it at any angle you please; and
in dealing with snakes this is an advantage. If Rikki-tikki had
only known, he was doing a much more dangerous thing than
fighting Nag, for Karait is so small and can turn so quickly that
unless Rikki bit him close to the back of the head, he would get
the return stroke in his eye or his lip. But Rikki did not know;
his eyes were all red, and he rocked back and forth, looking for
a good place to hold. Karait struck out, Rikki jumped sideways
and tried to run in, but the wicked little dusty gray head lashed
within a fraction of his shoulder, and he had to jump over the
body, and the head followed his heels close. **A**

Teddy shouted to the house: "Oh, look here! Our mongoose
is killing a snake," and Rikki-tikki heard a scream from Teddy's
mother. His father ran out with a stick, but by the time he
came up, Karait had lunged out once too far, and Rikki-tikki
had sprung, jumped on the snake's back, dropped his head far
between his forelegs, bitten as high up the back as he could get
hold, and rolled away. That bite paralyzed Karait, and Rikki-tikki
was just going to eat him up from the tail, after the custom of his
family at dinner, when he remembered that a full meal makes a

6. **gait** (GAYT) _n.:_ way of walking or running.

slow mongoose, and if he wanted all his strength and quickness
ready, he must keep himself thin. He went away for a dust bath
under the castor-oil bushes, while Teddy's father beat the dead

200   Karait. "What is the use of that?" thought Rikki-tikki; "I have
settled it all"; and then Teddy's mother picked him up from
the dust and hugged him, crying that he had saved Teddy from
death, and Teddy's father said that he was a providence,[7] and
Teddy looked on with big, scared eyes. Rikki-tikki was rather
amused at all the fuss, which, of course, he did not understand.
Teddy's mother might just as well have petted Teddy for playing
in the dust. Rikki was thoroughly enjoying himself. **B**

That night at dinner, walking to and fro among the wine-
glasses on the table, he might have stuffed himself three times

210   over with nice things; but he remembered Nag and Nagaina, and
though it was very pleasant to be patted and petted by Teddy's
mother and to sit on Teddy's shoulder, his eyes would get red
from time to time, and he would go off into his long war cry of
Rikk-tikk-tikki-tikki-tchk!

Teddy carried him off to bed and insisted on Rikki-tikki's sleeping under his chin. **C** Rikki-tikki was too well bred
to bite or scratch, but as soon as Teddy was asleep, he went off
for his nightly walk round the house, and in the dark he ran up
against Chuchundra, the muskrat, creeping round by the wall.

220   Chuchundra is a brokenhearted little beast. He whimpers and
cheeps all night, trying to make up his mind to run into the
middle of the room; but he never gets there.

"Don't kill me," said Chuchundra, almost weeping. "Rikki-
tikki, don't kill me!"

"Do you think a snake killer kills muskrats?" said Rikki-
tikki scornfully.

"Those who kill snakes get killed by snakes," said
Chuchundra, more sorrowfully than ever. "And how am I to be
sure that Nag won't mistake me for you some dark night?"

---

7. **providence** (PRAH VUH DEHNS) *n.:* favor or gift from God or nature.

B LITERARY FOCUS

How do Teddy's parents react to Rikki-tikki's **conflict** with Karait?

_____

_____

_____

_____

C READ AND DISCUSS

Comprehension
What does the family think of Rikki-tikki-tavi?

"There's not the least danger," said Rikki-tikki, "but Nag is in the garden, and I know you don't go there."

"My cousin Chua, the rat, told me—" said Chuchundra, and then he stopped.

"Told you what?"

"H'sh! Nag is everywhere, Rikki-tikki. You should have talked to Chua in the garden."

"I didn't—so you must tell me. Quick, Chuchundra, or I'll bite you!"

Chuchundra sat down and cried till the tears rolled off his whiskers. "I am a very poor man," he sobbed. "I never had spirit enough to run out into the middle of the room. H'sh! I mustn't tell you anything. Can't you *hear*, Rikki-tikki?"

Rikki-tikki listened. The house was as still as still, but he thought he could just catch the faintest *scratch-scratch* in the world—a noise as faint as that of a wasp walking on a windowpane—the dry scratch of a snake's scales on brickwork.

"That's Nag or Nagaina," he said to himself, "and he is crawling into the bathroom sluice.[8] You're right, Chuchundra; I should have talked to Chua." **A**

He stole off to Teddy's bathroom, but there was nothing there, and then to Teddy's mother's bathroom. At the bottom of the smooth plaster wall there was a brick pulled out to make a sluice for the bathwater, and as Rikki-tikki stole in by the masonry[9] curb where the bath is put, he heard Nag and Nagaina whispering together outside in the moonlight.

"When the house is emptied of people," said Nagaina to her husband, "*he* will have to go away, and then the garden will be our own again. Go in quietly, and remember that the big man who killed Karait is the first one to bite. Then come out and tell me, and we will hunt for Rikki-tikki together." **B**

"But are you sure that there is anything to be gained by killing the people?" said Nag.

---

8. **sluice** (SLOOS) *n.*: drain.
9. **masonry** *n.* used as *adj.*: something built of stone or brick.

"Everything. When there were no people in the bungalow, did we have any mongoose in the garden? So long as the bungalow is empty, we are king and queen of the garden; and remember that as soon as our eggs in the melon bed hatch (as they may tomorrow), our children will need room and quiet."

"I had not thought of that," said Nag. "I will go, but there is no need that we should hunt for Rikki-tikki afterward. I will kill the big man and his wife, and the child if I can, and come away quietly. Then the bungalow will be empty, and Rikki-tikki will go."

Rikki-tikki tingled all over with rage and hatred at this, and then Nag's head came through the sluice, and his five feet of cold body followed it. Angry as he was, Rikki-tikki was very frightened as he saw the size of the big cobra. Nag coiled himself up, raised his head, and looked into the bathroom in the dark, and Rikki could see his eyes glitter.

"Now, if I kill him here, Nagaina will know; and if I fight him on the open floor, the odds are in his favor. What am I to do?" said Rikki-tikki-tavi.

Nag waved to and fro, and then Rikki-tikki heard him drinking from the biggest water jar that was used to fill the bath. "That is good," said the snake. "Now, when Karait was killed, the big man had a stick. He may have that stick still, but when he comes in to bathe in the morning, he will not have a stick. I shall wait here till he comes. Nagaina—do you hear me?—I shall wait here in the cool till daytime." C

There was no answer from outside, so Rikki-tikki knew Nagaina had gone away. Nag coiled himself down, coil by coil, round the bulge at the bottom of the water jar, and Rikki-tikki stayed still as death. After an hour he began to move, muscle by muscle, toward the jar. Nag was asleep, and Rikki-tikki looked at his big back, wondering which would be the best place for a good hold. "If I don't break his back at the first jump," said Rikki, "he can still fight; and if he fights—O Rikki!" He looked at the thickness of the neck below the hood, but that was too much for him; and a bite near the tail would only make Nag savage.

270

280

290

Rikki is actually handling two **conflicts** here. In addition to fighting Nag, he faces a conflict with himself—he must overcome his fear. Which conflict do you think is more challenging for Rikki? Explain your answer.

_____

_____

_____

_____

_____

_____

_____

A **READ AND DISCUSS**

Comprehension

What has the author told us about Rikki-tikki's plan?

B **VOCABULARY**

Academic Vocabulary

How *accurate*, or free of error, was Rikki's attack?

300 "It must be the head," he said at last, "the head above the hood; and when I am once there, I must not let go." A

Then he jumped. The head was lying a little clear of the water jar, under the curve of it; and as his teeth met, Rikki braced his back against the bulge of the red earthenware to hold down the head. B This gave him just one second's purchase,[10] and he made the most of it. Then he was battered to and fro as a rat is shaken by a dog—to and fro on the floor, up and down, and round in great circles, but his eyes were red and he held on as the body cartwhipped over the floor, upsetting the tin dipper and the soap dish and the flesh brush, and banged against the
310 tin side of the bath. As he held, he closed his jaws tighter and tighter, for he made sure[11] he would be banged to death, and for the honor of his family, he preferred to be found with his teeth locked. He was dizzy, aching, and felt shaken to pieces, when something went off like a thunderclap just behind him; a hot wind knocked him senseless and red fire singed his fur. The big man had been wakened by the noise and had fired both barrels of a shotgun into Nag just behind the hood.

Rikki-tikki held on with his eyes shut, for now he was quite sure he was dead; but the head did not move, and the big man
320 picked him up and said: "It's the mongoose again, Alice; the little chap has saved *our* lives now." Then Teddy's mother came in with a very white face and saw what was left of Nag, and Rikki-tikki dragged himself to Teddy's bedroom and spent half the rest of the night shaking himself tenderly to find out whether he really was broken into forty pieces, as he fancied.

When morning came, he was very stiff but well pleased with his doings. "Now I have Nagaina to settle with, and she will be worse than five Nags, and there's no knowing when the eggs she spoke of will hatch. Goodness! I must go and see Darzee,"
330 he said.

Without waiting for breakfast, Rikki-tikki ran to the thorn bush, where Darzee was singing a song of triumph at the top of

---

10. **purchase** *n.*: firm hold.
11. **made sure**: here, felt sure.

his voice. The news of Nag's death was all over the garden, for the sweeper had thrown the body on the rubbish heap.

"Oh, you stupid tuft of feathers!" said Rikki-tikki angrily. "Is this the time to sing?"

"Nag is dead—is dead—is dead!" sang Darzee. "The valiant Rikki-tikki caught him by the head and held fast. **C** The big man brought the bang-stick, and Nag fell in two pieces! He will
340   never eat my babies again."

"All that's true enough, but where's Nagaina?" said Rikki-tikki, looking carefully round him.

"Nagaina came to the bathroom sluice and called for Nag," Darzee went on; "and Nag came out on the end of a stick—the sweeper picked him up on the end of a stick and threw him upon the rubbish heap. Let us sing about the great, the red-eyed Rikki-tikki!" and Darzee filled his throat and sang.

"If I could get up to your nest, I'd roll your babies out!" said Rikki-tikki. "You don't know when to do the right thing at the
350   right time. You're safe enough in your nest there, but it's war for me down here. Stop singing a minute, Darzee."

"For the great, beautiful Rikki-tikki's sake I will stop," said Darzee. "What is it, O Killer of the terrible Nag?"

"Where is Nagaina, for the third time?"

"On the rubbish heap by the stables, mourning for Nag. Great is Rikki-tikki with the white teeth."

"Bother[12] my white teeth! Have you ever heard where she keeps her eggs?"

"In the melon bed, on the end nearest the wall, where the
360   sun strikes nearly all day. She hid them there weeks ago."

"And you never thought it worthwhile to tell me? The end nearest the wall, you said?"

"Rikki-tikki, you are not going to eat her eggs?"

"Not eat exactly; no. Darzee, if you have a grain of sense, you will fly off to the stables and pretend that your wing is broken and let Nagaina chase you away to this bush. I must get to the melon bed, and if I went there now, she'd see me." **D**

---

12. **bother** *interj.:* here, never mind.

C VOCABULARY

Selection Vocabulary
How would you describe Rikki's personality? Considering Rikki's actions and personality, what do you think *valiant* means?

_____

_____

_____

_____

_____

_____

D READ AND DISCUSS

Comprehension
Why does Rikki-tikki want Darzee to pretend his wing is broken?

A **READ AND DISCUSS**

Comprehension
Darzee is supposed to have the broken wing. Why is his wife pretending to have one?

B **LANGUAGE COACH**

Selection Vocabulary
The Latin word *consolari* means "to offer comfort." Circle the word in this sentence that comes from this Latin **word root**.

_____

_____

_____

_____

_____

_____

370 Darzee was a featherbrained little fellow who could never hold more than one idea at a time in his head, and just because he knew that Nagaina's children were born in eggs like his own, he didn't think at first that it was fair to kill them. But his wife was a sensible bird, and she knew that cobra's eggs meant young cobras later on; so she flew off from the nest and left Darzee to keep the babies warm and continue his song about the death of Nag. Darzee was very like a man in some ways.

She fluttered in front of Nagaina by the rubbish heap and cried out, "Oh, my wing is broken! The boy in the house threw a stone at me and broke it." Then she fluttered more desperately than ever. A

380 Nagaina lifted up her head and hissed, "You warned Rikki-tikki when I would have killed him. Indeed and truly, you've chosen a bad place to be lame in." And she moved toward Darzee's wife, slipping along over the dust.

"The boy broke it with a stone!" shrieked Darzee's wife.

"Well! It may be some consolation to you when you're dead to know that I shall settle accounts with the boy. B My husband lies on the rubbish heap this morning, but before night the boy in the house will lie very still. What is the use of running away? I am sure to catch you. Little fool, look at me!"

390 Darzee's wife knew better than to do *that*, for a bird who looks at a snake's eyes gets so frightened that she cannot move. Darzee's wife fluttered on, piping sorrowfully and never leaving the ground, and Nagaina quickened her pace.

Rikki-tikki heard them going up the path from the stables, and he raced for the end of the melon patch near the wall. There, in the warm litter above the melons, very cunningly hidden, he found twenty-five eggs about the size of a bantam's[13] eggs but with whitish skins instead of shells.

"I was not a day too soon," he said, for he could see the
400 baby cobras curled up inside the skin, and he knew that the minute they were hatched, they could each kill a man or a

---

13. **bantam's:** small chicken's.

© K. Senani/OSF/Animals Animals–Earth Scenes

C READING FOCUS

Summarize how Rikki managed to break nearly all of Nagaina's eggs.

mongoose. He bit off the tops of the eggs as fast as he could, taking care to crush the young cobras, and turned over the litter from time to time to see whether he had missed any. At last there were only three eggs left, and Rikki-tikki began to chuckle to himself, when he heard Darzee's wife screaming: **C**

"Rikki-tikki, I led Nagaina toward the house, and she has gone into the veranda, and—oh, come quickly—she means killing!" **D**

410   Rikki-tikki smashed two eggs, and tumbled backward down the melon bed with the third egg in his mouth, and scuttled to the veranda as hard as he could put foot to the ground. Teddy and his mother and father were there at early breakfast, but Rikki-tikki saw that they were not eating anything. They sat stone still, and their faces were white. Nagaina was coiled up on the matting by Teddy's chair, within easy striking distance of Teddy's bare leg, and she was swaying to and fro, singing a song of triumph. **E**

"Son of the big man that killed Nag," she hissed, "stay still.
420   I am not ready yet. Wait a little. Keep very still, all you three! If you move, I strike, and if you do not move, I strike. Oh, foolish people, who killed my Nag!"

D READ AND DISCUSS

Comprehension
How are things looking for the family? What is Rikki-tikki up to?

E LITERARY FOCUS

While Rikki destroys Nagaina's eggs, a new **conflict** arises. What problem does Rikki face now?

A **READING FOCUS**

What is the **main idea** of this paragraph?

_____

_____

_____

_____

_____

_____

_____

B **READ AND DISCUSS**

Comprehension

What do you learn about Nagaina here?

Teddy's eyes were fixed on his father, and all his father could do was to whisper, "Sit still, Teddy. You mustn't move. Teddy, keep still."

Then Rikki-tikki came up and cried: "Turn round, Nagaina; turn and fight!"

"All in good time," said she, without moving her eyes. "I will settle my account with *you* presently. Look at your friends, Rikki-tikki. They are still and white. They are afraid. They dare not move, and if you come a step nearer, I strike."

"Look at your eggs," said Rikki-tikki, "in the melon bed near the wall. Go and look, Nagaina!"

The big snake turned half round and saw the egg on the veranda. "Ah-h! Give it to me," she said.

Rikki-tikki put his paws one on each side of the egg, and his eyes were blood-red. "What price for a snake's egg? For a young cobra? For a young king cobra? For the last—the very last of the brood? The ants are eating all the others down by the melon bed." **A**

Nagaina spun clear round, forgetting everything for the sake of the one egg; and Rikki-tikki saw Teddy's father shoot out a big hand, catch Teddy by the shoulder, and drag him across the little table with the teacups, safe and out of reach of Nagaina.

"Tricked! Tricked! Tricked! *Rikk-tck-tck!*" chuckled Rikki-tikki. "The boy is safe, and it was I—I—I—that caught Nag by the hood last night in the bathroom." Then he began to jump up and down, all four feet together, his head close to the floor. "He threw me to and fro, but he could not shake me off. He was dead before the big man blew him in two. I did it! *Rikki-tikki-tck-tck!* Come then, Nagaina. Come and fight with me. You shall not be a widow long."

Nagaina saw that she had lost her chance of killing Teddy, and the egg lay between Rikki-tikki's paws. "Give me the egg, Rikki-tikki. Give me the last of my eggs, and I will go away and never come back," she said, lowering her hood. **B**

"Yes, you will go away, and you will never come back; for you will go to the rubbish heap with Nag. Fight, widow! The big man has gone for his gun! Fight!"

460   Rikki-tikki was bounding all round Nagaina, keeping just out of reach of her stroke, his little eyes like hot coals. Nagaina gathered herself together and flung out at him. Rikki-tikki jumped up and backwards. Again and again and again she struck, and each time her head came with a whack on the matting of the veranda and she gathered herself together like a watch spring. Then Rikki-tikki danced in a circle to get behind her, and Nagaina spun round to keep her head to his head, so that the rustle of her tail on the matting sounded like dry leaves blown along by the wind. **C**

470   He had forgotten the egg. It still lay on the veranda, and Nagaina came nearer and nearer to it, till at last, while Rikki-tikki was drawing breath, she caught it in her mouth, turned to the veranda steps, and flew like an arrow down the path, with Rikki-tikki behind her. When the cobra runs for her life, she goes like a whiplash flicked across a horse's neck. Rikki-tikki knew that he must catch her or all the trouble would begin again. She headed straight for the long grass by the thorn bush, and as he was running, Rikki-tikki heard Darzee still singing his foolish little song of triumph. But Darzee's wife was wiser.

480   She flew off her nest as Nagaina came along and flapped her wings about Nagaina's head. If Darzee had helped, they might have turned her, but Nagaina only lowered her hood and went on. Still, the instant's delay brought Rikki-tikki up to her, and as she plunged into the rat hole where she and Nag used to live, his little white teeth were clenched on her tail and he went down with her—and very few mongooses, however wise and old they may be, care to follow a cobra into its hole. It was dark in the hole, and Rikki-tikki never knew when it might open out and give Nagaina room to turn and strike at him. He held on

490   savagely and stuck out his feet to act as brakes on the dark slope of the hot, moist earth. Then the grass by the mouth of the hole

In this **conflict** between Rikki and Nagaina, who do you think has the advantage? Why?

_____

_____

_____

_____

_____

Academic Vocabulary

For protecting the family in the future, why is it *significant,* or important, that Rikki should destroy the cobras' eggs in addition to killing Nag and Nagaina?

_____
_____
_____
_____
_____
_____

B **READING FOCUS**

Summarize the events that take place in this paragraph.

_____
_____
_____
_____
_____
_____
_____
_____
_____
_____
_____

stopped waving, and Darzee said: "It is all over with Rikki-tikki! We must sing his death song. Valiant Rikki-tikki is dead! For Nagaina will surely kill him underground." **A** **B**

So he sang a very mournful song that he made up on the spur of the minute, and just as he got to the most touching part, the grass quivered again, and Rikki-tikki, covered with dirt, dragged himself out of the hole leg by leg, licking his whiskers. Darzee stopped with a little shout. Rikki-tikki shook some of
500 the dust out of his fur and sneezed. "It is all over," he said. "The widow will never come out again." And the red ants that live between the grass stems heard him and began to troop down one after another to see if he had spoken the truth.

Rikki-tikki curled himself up in the grass and slept where he was—slept and slept till it was late in the afternoon, for he had done a hard day's work.

"Now," he said, when he awoke, "I will go back to the house. Tell the Coppersmith, Darzee, and he will tell the garden that Nagaina is dead."
510 The Coppersmith is a bird who makes a noise exactly like the beating of a little hammer on a copper pot; and the reason he is always making it is because he is the town crier to every Indian garden and tells all the news to everybody who cares to listen. As Rikki-tikki went up the path, he heard his "attention" notes like a tiny dinner gong and then the steady "*Ding-dong-tock!* Nag is dead—*dong!* Nagaina is dead! *Ding-dong-tock!*" That set all the birds in the garden singing and the frogs croaking, for Nag and Nagaina used to eat frogs as well as little birds.
520 When Rikki got to the house, Teddy and Teddy's mother (she looked very white still, for she had been fainting) and Teddy's father came out and almost cried over him; and that night he ate all that was given him till he could eat no more and went to bed on Teddy's shoulder, where Teddy's mother saw him when she came to look late at night.

"He saved our lives and Teddy's life," she said to her husband. "Just think, he saved all our lives." **C**

Rikki-tikki woke up with a jump, for the mongooses are light sleepers.

530 "Oh, it's you," said he. "What are you bothering for? All the cobras are dead; and if they weren't, I'm here."

Rikki-tikki had a right to be proud of himself, but he did not grow too proud, and he kept that garden as a mongoose should keep it, with tooth and jump and spring and bite, till never a cobra dared show its head inside the walls.

Darzee's Chant

Sung in honor of Rikki-tikki-tavi

Singer and tailor am I—
    Doubled the joys that I know—
Proud of my lilt[14] to the sky,
    Proud of the house that I sew.
540 Over and under, so weave I my music—
    so weave I the house that I sew.

Sing to your fledglings[15] again,
    Mother, O lift up your head!
Evil that plagued us is slain,
    Death in the garden lies dead.
Terror that hid in the roses is impotent—
    flung on the dunghill and dead!
Who has delivered us, who?
550   Tell me his nest and his name.
Rikki, the valiant, the true,
    Tikki, with eyeballs of flame—
Rikk-tikki-tikki, the ivory-fanged,
    the hunter with eyeballs of flame!

14. **lilt** *n.*: song.
15. **fledglings** (FLEHJ LINGZ) *n.*: baby birds.

C READ AND DISCUSS

Comprehension
What does the family think of Rikki-tikki-tavi now?

A (READ AND DISCUSS)

Comprehension
What is the purpose of
Darzee's chant?

Give him the Thanks of the Birds,
    Bowing with tail feathers spread,
Praise him with nightingale words—
    Nay, I will praise him instead.
Hear! I will sing you the praise of the
560   bottle-tailed Rikki with eyeballs of red!

*(Here Rikki-tikki interrupted, so the rest
of the song is lost.).* **A**

Applying Your Skills

Rikki-tikki-tavi

VOCABULARY DEVELOPMENT

DIRECTIONS: Choose the vocabulary word from the Word Box that correctly completes each sentence. Not every word will be used.

Word Box

immensely

cowered

valiant

consolation

1. Darzee _____ in his nest whenever Nag approached.

2. Rikki's courage helped him become a _____ hero.

3. After Rikki saved Teddy's life, the family appreciated him _____.

LITERARY FOCUS: CONFLICT

DIRECTIONS: Write "Yes" after each sentence below if it is an example of **conflict** in "Rikki-tikki-tavi." Write "No" if it is not.

1. Darzee and his wife build a nest by stitching two big leaves together.

_____

2. Rikki must protect Teddy from Karait, a deadly snake.

_____

3. Teddy's dad shoots Nag while Rikki is attacking him.

_____

READING FOCUS: SUMMARIZING

DIRECTIONS: Summarizing the major events is a good way to better understand and appreciate a story. Copy and complete the chart below by summarizing the climax (most exciting part) and resolution (solution to the conflict) of "Rikki-tikki-tavi."

Major Conflict: Nag and Nagaina plan to kill Teddy and his family so they can have the yard to themselves to raise their babies.

↓

1. Climax:

↓

2. Resolution:

SKILLS FOCUS

Literary Skills
Examine conflicts that characters face.

Reading Skills
Summarize a text.

Flea Patrol, The Black Death, On Preventing Plague, and Signs

INFORMATIONAL TEXT FOCUS: STRUCTURE OF NEWSPAPER ARTICLES, TEXT BOOKS, INSTRUCTION MANUALS, AND SIGNS

It is important to understand the **purpose**, **main idea**, and **structure** of informational sources. The chart below shows what kind of structure, or organization, you would find in some of these sources.

Newspaper Article	Textbook	Instructional Manual	Signs
Headline	Table of contents	Table of contents	Symbols
Subhead	Section preview and summary	Steps	Images
Byline	Captions	Diagrams	Colors
Dateline		Glossary	
Lead		Index	

SELECTION VOCABULARY

transmitted (TRANS MIHT IHD) *v.:* caused to pass from one thing to another.
> *Fleas that fed on rats transmitted the plague throughout Europe.*

application (AP LUH KAY SHUHN) *n.:* act of putting to use.
> *An application of insecticide kills fleas.*

rural (RUR UHL) *adj.:* of or relating to the countryside.
> *People living in rural areas are at greater risk of catching the plague.*

WORD STUDY

DIRECTIONS: Fill in the correct vocabulary words to complete the paragraph.

Today the plague is more likely to be (1) _____ to people in (2) _____ areas. The (3) _____ of pesticides can help kill the fleas that carry the disease.

SKILLS FOCUS

Informational Text Skills
Understand the structure and purpose of informational readings.

FLEA PATROL: KEEPING NATIONAL PARKS SAFE FROM PLAGUE

by Jessica Cohn

BACKGROUND
This newspaper article describes how scientists and park rangers are trying to keep U.S. national parks safe from the threat of bubonic plague.

BLANDING, UTAH, January 10—Park rangers are hunting fleas to stop the spread of disease. They are on alert to fight a plague of rodents in some national parks. **A**

Bubonic plague is found in rodents and their fleas in several areas of the United States, including some national parks. To keep things under control, rangers spray insecticide. They hope to kill fleas, which can spread the disease to humans. But before you scratch an overnight park visit off your list of things to do, you should know something else. No humans have ever been

10   known to be infected with plague at national park campgrounds. With this course of action, officials are just planning to keep it that way. **B**

At least a third of Europeans died from the plague during the Middle Ages. That deadly drama, known as the "Black

A READING FOCUS

Based on this opening paragraph, called the **lead**, what is the topic of this newspaper article?

_____

_____

B READING FOCUS

What is the **main idea**, or central point, of this paragraph?

_____

_____

_____

_____

_____

_____

_____

Microscopic flea © E. Pollard/
PhotoLink/Getty Images

What is the author's **purpose**, or reason, for including this information from Ralph Jones?

_____

_____

_____

_____

B (READ AND DISCUSS)

Comprehension

What has the author set up for you? **Follow-up:** Why might park rangers worry about this news getting out to the public?

C (LANGUAGE COACH)

Word Study

The word *antibiotics* comes from the Greek words *anti* (meaning "against") and *biotikos* (meaning "of or relating to life"). Which "life" are the antibiotics fighting against—the life of humans or the life of the germs that make up the plague? Explain.

_____

_____

_____

_____

_____

_____

Death," is kept alive in history, literature, and imagination. "As soon as people hear 'Black Death' or 'plague,' they freak out," says Ralph Jones, manager of National Bridges National Park in Utah. "But that's not the way it is anymore. It's just a naturally occurring disease. It's just part of the world." **A**

20   In spring 2006, rangers discovered more dead field mice and kangaroo rats at National Bridges than was normal. Curious as to the reason, the rangers had the animals tested at the Centers for Disease Control and Prevention, a federal agency responsible for protecting the health and safety of the population. The plague bacterium was uncovered. **B**

National Bridges closed its campground until the disease could be contained. Sites reopened that May. The same year, plague was found among creatures in Mesa Verde National Park and Colorado National Monument, reported the U.S. Public

30   Health Service.

"Bubonic plague goes in cycles," says Jones, "depending on the population of the rodents."

People get sick when bitten by fleas that have chomped on rodents carrying the bacterium. The disease can also be transmitted through contact with infected sores or by breathing infected matter in the air. Plague can be cured as long as humans seek medical help and are treated with antibiotics. **C** But every year, countless rodents die from the disease.

Officials who find infection among animals concentrate

40   on killing off fleas. An application of insecticide at rodent holes is recommended when dead animals are identified as plague carriers.

The disease is regularly found in creatures throughout the western United States, especially the area known as Four Corners, where the states of Arizona, Colorado, New Mexico, and Utah meet. Prairie dogs are also known to be carriers. The trick is keeping the disease contained to wild animals, which is usually easy enough. Most people avoid contact with these creatures.

50   About ten to fifteen bubonic plague cases are reported in humans yearly in the United States, mostly in rural areas, says the Centers for Disease Control and Prevention. One in seven cases is fatal. The southeastern United States is especially affected. Africa, Asia, and South America have hot spots as well. In 2006, a Los Angeles woman was treated for the disease, that area's first case in over twenty years. **D**

    Researchers at the University of Oslo recently studied field data on creatures known as great gerbils, along with related weather records. Plague increased more than 50 percent among

60 the animals with temperature increases of fewer than 2 degrees Fahrenheit.

Bubonic Plague Symptoms **E**

Bubonic plague is treatable with antibiotics. Symptoms show two to seven days after infection:

- blackish-purple lumps under skin
- chills
- diarrhea
- exhaustion
- fever
- headache
70 - muscle pain
- tender, swollen lymph nodes
- vomiting

D READ AND DISCUSS

Comprehension

The author gave us a lot of examples here. What do all these instances of bubonic plague show us?

E READING FOCUS

Why are plague symptoms shown as bulleted text in a box? How does this **structure** draw attention to the information?

_____

_____

_____

_____

THE BLACK DEATH

from World History: Medieval to Early Modern Times

BACKGROUND

The following pages are taken from a world history textbook. They use a combination of pictures and words to describe the Black Death, a deadly plague that hit Europe between 1347 and 1351. Millions of people died from the disease. Read on to see how the Black Death affected the society and economy of Europe.

A **READING FOCUS**

What does this **table of contents** tell you about the topics covered in Chapter 10 of this textbook?

_____

_____

_____

_____

B **READING FOCUS**

Based on this **table of contents**, what skills are students expected to practice in this chapter?

_____

_____

CHAPTER 10 **The Later Middle Ages** 256

California Standards

History–Social Science
7.6 Students analyze the geographic, political, economic, religious, and social structures of the civilizations of Medieval Europe.

Analysis Skills
CS 3 Identify physical and cultural features.
HI 2 Understand and distinguish cause and effect.

History's Impact Video Series
The Bubonic Plague

XV Contents

The Black Death

While the English and French fought the Hundred Years' War, an even greater crisis arose. This crisis was the **Black Death**, a deadly plague that swept through Europe between 1347 and 1351.

The plague originally came from central and eastern Asia. Unknowingly, traders brought rats carrying the disease to Mediterranean ports in 1347. From there it quickly swept throughout much of Europe. Fleas that feasted on the blood of infected rats passed on the plague to people.

C

The Black Death was not caused by one disease but by several different forms of plague. One form called bubonic plague (byoo-BAH-nik PLAYG) could be identified by swellings called buboes that appeared on victims' bodies. Another even deadlier form could spread through the air and kill people in less than a day.

The Black Death killed so many people that many were buried quickly without priests or ceremonies. In some villages nearly everyone died or fled as neighbors fell ill. In England alone, about 1,000 villages were abandoned.

D

The plague killed millions of people in Europe and millions more around the world. Some historians think Europe lost about a third of its population—perhaps 25 million people. This huge drop in population caused sweeping changes in Europe.

In most places, the manor system fell apart completely. There weren't enough people left to work in the fields. Those peasants and serfs who had survived the plague found their skills in high demand. Suddenly, they could demand wages for their labor. Once they had money, many fled their manors completely, moving instead to Europe's growing cities.

E

READING CHECK Identifying Cause and Effect What effects did bubonic plague have in Europe?

SUMMARY AND PREVIEW Magna Carta, the Hundred Years' War, and the Black Death changed European society. In the next section, you will learn about other changes in society, changes brought about by religious differences.

Section 4 Assessment

go.hrw.com
Online Quiz
KEYWORD: SQ7 HP10

Reviewing Ideas, Terms, and People HSS 7.6.5, 7.6.7

1. **a. Identify** What document did English nobles hope would limit the king's power?
   b. Explain How was the creation of **Parliament** a step toward the creation of democracy in England?
2. **a. Identify** Who rallied the French troops during the **Hundred Years' War**?
   b. Elaborate The Hundred Years' War caused much more damage in France than in England. Why do you think this was the case?
3. **a. Describe** What was the **Black Death**?
   b. Explain How did the Black Death contribute to the decline of the manor system?
   c. Elaborate Why do you think the Black Death was able to spread so quickly through Europe?

Critical Thinking

4. **Identifying Cause and Effect** Draw a scroll like the one shown here. Inside the scroll, list two ideas contained in Magna Carta. Next to the scroll, write two sentences about Magna Carta's effects on England's government.

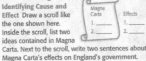

Magna Carta
1. _____
2. _____

Effects
1. _____
2. _____

FOCUS ON WRITING

5. **Rating Importance** After reading this section, you'll probably want to add King John to your list. You should also start to think about which people were the most important. Rank the people on your list from most to least important.

C — VOCABULARY

Word Study

Find a synonym (word with a similar meaning) for *plague* in this paragraph and write it below.

_____

D — READ AND DISCUSS

Comprehension

How did the world deal with the Black Death?

E — READ AND DISCUSS

Comprehension

How does the idea of peasants moving into cities fit into the picture of the Black Death?

Comprehension

What does the graphic help us understand?

This image of a rat is an example of an **inset**, a smaller image placed inside a larger picture. How does this inset add information to this graphic?

_____

_____

_____

_____

History and Geography

The Black Death

A

"And they died by the hundreds," wrote one man who saw the horror, "both day and night." The Black Death had arrived. The Black Death was a series of deadly plagues that hit Europe between 1347 and 1351, killing millions. People didn't know what caused the plague. They also didn't know that geography played a key role in its spread—as people traveled to trade, they unwittingly carried the disease with them to new places.

EUROPE

CENTRAL ASIA

Kaffa

CHINA

AFRICA

The plague probably began in central and eastern Asia. These arrows show how it spread into and through Europe.

B

This ship has just arrived in Europe from the east with trade goods—and rats with fleas.

The fleas carry the plague and jump onto a man unloading the ship. Soon, he will get sick and die.

280

The plague is so terrifying that many people think it's the end of the world. They leave town for the country, spreading the Black Death even farther.

People dig mass graves to bury the dead. But often, so many victims are infected that there is no one left to bury them.

The garbage and dirty conditions in the town provide food and a home for the rats, allowing the disease to spread even more.

So many people die so quickly that special carts are sent through the streets to gather the bodies.

GEOGRAPHY SKILLS **INTERPRETING MAPS**
1. How did the Black Death reach Europe from Asia?
2. What helped spread the plague within Europe?

281

How do the **captions** help you understand what is taking place? Would you be able to understand the graphic without the captions?

_____

_____

_____

_____

What part of this graphic is meant to help you review the **main ideas** you have learned?

_____

_____

_____

_____

ON PREVENTING PLAGUE

BACKGROUND

This selection is a mock manual for preventing the spread of bubonic plague. It is based on an actual manual from the seventeenth century. Such manuals offered advice to people on how to stop the spread of plague. However, since this advice was based on the limited medical knowledge of the time, it was not always effective.

A VOCABULARY

Word Study

You can often learn the meaning of an unfamiliar word by looking at the words that come after it. What word here gives you a clue to the meaning of the word *infection*?

B READING FOCUS

According to this **table of contents**, what are the first and last steps that should be taken to prevent the spread of plague?

ON PREVENTING PLAGUE

CONTENTS

Steps to Prevent Spread of Infection

1. Notice of the Sickness **A**
2. Every Visited House to Be Marked
3. Every Visited House to Be Watched
4. Shutting Up of Infected Houses; Isolation of Villages
5. Airing Out of the Stuff
6. No Infectious Stuff
7. Burial of the Dead
8. Protection for Physicians **B**

ON PREVENTING PLAGUE

by  THE WORLD ALMANAC

Read with a Purpose
Read this adaptation of an instructional manual to learn how people living in the seventeenth century dealt with outbreaks of plague.

— July 6, 1665 —

BY THE ORDER OF THE LORD ARLINGTON,
SECRETARY OF STATE TO HIS MAJESTY,
KING CHARLES II OF ENGLAND,

I am commanded to publish the following instructions:

Steps to Prevent Spread of Infection

1. Notice of the Sickness
The master of every house shall give notice to the health examiner within two hours of seeing a sign of the sickness on any person in the house. Signs include a pimple or a swelling in any body part. Anyone falling dangerously sick shall be reported.

2. Every Visited House to Be Marked
Every house visited by the illness must be clearly marked with a red cross. This will be one foot long and in the middle of the door. The cross must remain until the lawful opening of the house. **D**

3. Every Visited House to Be Watched
The constable must see that every house with the illness remains shut up. The visited houses will be guarded by watchmen. The watchmen will bring the inhabitants necessities at their own cost. This will last until four weeks after all in the house become well. **E**

4. Shutting Up of Infected Houses; Isolation of Villages
The house of anyone who has entered any infected house will be shut up for a number of days. This number will be decided by the examiner. No person, infected or otherwise, shall leave the infected houses.

APPOINTED OFFICERS **C**

Examiners: The examiners shall learn which houses have been visited by illness. If they find any person sick, they shall give orders that the house be shut up. (If any fit examiner fails to do his duty, he will be sent to prison.)

Watchmen: Every affected house shall be assigned two watchmen, one for day and the other for night. The watchmen must take care that no person goes into or out of the house.

Searchers: Women searchers of honest reputation shall be appointed. They shall swear to search for persons dying of plague. They will give true report of their findings.

Nurse Keepers: Before any nurse keeper leaves an infected house, a number of days must be passed. If she leaves before twenty-eight days after the death of any infected person, the next house she attends will be shut up. It will be shut up until twenty-eight days have passed.

C VOCABULARY

Word Study
The word *appointed* means "chosen for a job." These officers were given their positions by other officials. What word would you use to describe people who are put in office by popular vote?

_____

D READING FOCUS

Read the first two **steps** given. According to these instructions, what should you do when someone in your house is sick?

_____

_____

_____

_____

E READING FOCUS

Underline the details here that support the **main idea** of step 4.

Beak (primitive gas mask), filled with *spices and herbs*

Mouth, nose, and **ears** stuffed with *garlic and incense*

Total coverage, to prevent *flea bites*

Outer coat, *coated in wax*

READING FOCUS

Read this **caption** carefully. What details does it tell you about the purpose of the garment?

_____

_____

_____

_____

B READ AND DISCUSS

Comprehension

What does this picture let us know?

C VOCABULARY

Word Study

What two synonyms for *clothing* are listed in step 6?

_____

_____

If any person leaves an infected village, he will be brought back by night. He will be punished by the constable. All public assemblies are forbidden during this visit by the plague.

5. Airing Out of the Stuff

The goods and clothing of the infected must be well aired with fire and perfumes. The bedding and apparel of the infected will be treated in the same manner.

6. No Infectious Stuff

No clothes, bedding, or garments shall be removed from any infected house. The sale of secondhand clothing and bedding is prohibited, on pain of imprisonment. If any buyer takes bedding or apparel from any seller's house within two months after an infection, the buyer's house will be shut up. This shall last a minimum of twenty days. C

7. Burial of the Dead

The burial of the dead killed by this plague will be carried out before the sun rises or after the sun sets. This will be done with the knowledge of the constables. No neighbors or friends are allowed to take the corpse to church. No one will enter a home visited by the illness. In doing so,

Dr. Schnabel of Rome, a plague doctor in 1656 by Paul Fuerst. Copper engraving.

B

he risks having his house shut up or imprisonment. No children are allowed to come near the corpse, coffin, or grave. They will keep their distance at the burial of any corpse in any church, churchyard, or burying place. All graves will be at least six feet deep.

8. Protection for Physicians

Physicians treating the infected will wear proper garb. The bronze mask, shaped like a beak, will cover the head completely. It will be filled with medicines and herbs that clean the bad air that causes infection. The physician will place garlic in his mouth and incense in his nose and ears. An outer cloak coated in wax will be worn whenever treating an ill person.

SIGNS

What would clue you in to the fact that this sign means "danger"?

Which sign means "dogs are allowed"? Which sign means "no dogs allowed"? What symbol gives you that information?

A

Imagine that you have arrived for the first time in Mexico City. If you need information, would these signs help you? What clues give you your answer? Why wouldn't the second sign work in every country?

B

What does this **symbol** mean? How do you know? Why might this sign pose a problem for someone who is not familiar with ancient mythology?

B READING FOCUS

What **main idea** is this **sign** communicating? Why do you think signs do not include details?

_____

_____

_____

_____

 C VOCABULARY

Word Study

Biohazard is a compound word. It comes from the Latin _bios_, or life, and _hazard_, meaning risk. What other kinds of _hazards_ might a sign warn you about?

_____

_____

_____

_____

When you travel, you might need a drugstore. If you know about Greek mythology, you can describe what this universal symbol for "pharmacy" means. **A**

If you were driving along a road and saw this sign, would you continue? Why or why not?

Signs say a great deal with only a simple graphic or illustration. What does this sign say to you? **B**

Here is a familiar sign. What is it saying?

Do you know what this sign means? It's the biohazard symbol, which warns people that something is a biological agent that is dangerous to humans or the environment. The biohazard symbol did not have a distinct meaning when it was created, but it is memorable. Its creators wanted to educate people on the meaning of a new, standardized symbol.

 **C**

Applying Your Skills

Flea Patrol, The Black Death, On Preventing Plague, *and* Signs

VOCABULARY DEVELOPMENT

DIRECTIONS: Write the correct vocabulary word from the Word Box on the blank to complete each sentence. One word will be used twice.

Word Box

application

rural

transmitted

1. The message was _____ using Morse code.

2. The family was not used to the big city, having moved from a _____ area.

3. No one knew that fleas _____ the illness.

4. This problem calls for the _____ of what we have learned in class.

INFORMATIONAL TEXT FOCUS: STRUCTURE OF NEWSPAPER ARTICLES, TEXTBOOKS, INSTRUCTION MANUALS, AND SIGNS

DIRECTIONS: Using the notes you have taken on the four informational readings, create a **table of contents** for the entire collection. In your table of contents, list the titles of the main readings. Include a **heading** that tells what the purpose of each article is. Beneath the heading for each article, list the article's **main ideas**. Use the following mock table of contents for "Flea Patrol" as a guide. The words in parentheses will help you get organized.

Table of Contents

(Title)   (Purpose of article)

Flea Patrol:

(Main ideas)

— Fighting the Plague in U.S. National Parks

— Details on the Modern Plague

— The Symptoms of Bubonic Plague

SKILLS FOCUS

Informational Text Skills
Understand the structure and purpose of informational readings.

Collection 2

VOCABULARY REVIEW

DIRECTIONS: For each of the words below, write down the vocabulary word from the Word Box that means the opposite.

Word Box

accurate

adequate

application

consolation

cowered

immensely

rural

similar

significant

transmitted

valiant

1. unlike: _____

2. cowardly: _____

3. false: _____

4. insufficient: _____

5. braved: _____

DIRECTIONS: Fill in the blanks with words from the Word Box that best fit the meaning of each sentence. You will not use all of the words in the Word Box. No words will be used more than once.

The Black Death had a (6) _____ effect on Europe. The disease was (7) _____ very quickly. Not even people living in (8) _____ areas were safe. It was hard to get (9) _____ information about the plague. As a result, people were (10) _____ frightened. At the time, there were no (11) _____ treatments for the disease. Being around the sick was very dangerous. The (12) _____ people who cared for the sick thus showed great bravery. After the Black Death, the increased number of jobs for the survivors was a small (13) _____ for the terrors they had faced.

Skills Practice

Collection 2

LANGUAGE COACH

DIRECTIONS: Many English words have affixes, or word parts that are added to the beginning or end of a word to change its meaning. Many of these affixes come from Latin. Match the Latin affixes below with their meanings. If you are stuck, you can use a dictionary to help you.

1. _____ pre-
2. _____ post-
3. _____ trans-
4. _____ -ation
5. _____ sub-

a. across
b. the act of
c. before
d. after
e. below

WRITING ACTIVITY

DIRECTIONS: Informational articles can come in many different forms such as newspaper articles, textbooks, manuals, and signs. A warning poster is another kind of informational text. Use the information from the sources in this collection to create a poster that warns people about the bubonic plague. Your poster should briefly describe the dangers of the plague, provide some information about how it is spread, and suggest some ways to avoid catching it. Stick to main ideas and be brief about each point. If your poster is too large or has too many words, it will be difficult for people to read. Include a bold title and at least one appropriate warning sign or graphic on your poster to help catch people's attention.

Character

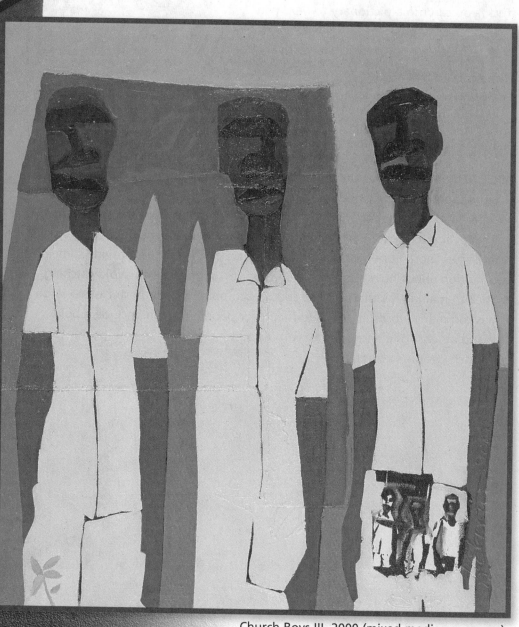

Church Boys III, 2000 (mixed media on canvas),
Deceus, Francks/Private Collection/
The Bridgeman Art Library International

Literary and Academic Vocabulary for Collection 3

attribute (AT RUH BYOOT) *n.:* quality or trait of someone or something.

One attribute of the narrator is that he is shy around girls.

identify (Y DEHN TUH FY) *v.:* to recognize and be able to say what someone or something is.

When you can identify a character's motivation, you gain insights into the character's behavior.

process (PRAHS EHS) *n.:* a series of actions or steps toward a goal.

Characterization is a process of revealing what characters are like.

respond (RIH SPAHND) *v.:* to act in return; to reply.

You respond to details about a character by making inferences about them.

character traits (KAR IHK TUHR TRAYTS) *n.:* ways to describe the personalities of people in a story.

In the book I just read, the character traits of the main character included a good sense of humor and an outgoing personality.

characterization (KAR IHK TUHR Y ZAY SHUHN) *n.:* the process of revealing a character's traits in a story.

Through characterization, the author showed us that Bobby was a very patient person.

The War of the Wall

by Toni Cade Bambara

LITERARY FOCUS: MOTIVATION

The reason behind a character's actions is called the character's **motivation**. As you read, ask yourself: what makes the characters act the way they do? How do their actions help you understand what the characters are like?

Why? Think of a character from one of your favorite stories or films. List three of that character's actions in the left column of the chart below. Then, in the right column, put a possible motivation for each action. If you are having trouble coming up with the motivation, ask yourself: Why did the character do that? Your answer is likely to be the motivation.

Name of the Character: _____	
Character's Actions	**Motivation for this Action**

SKILLS FOCUS

Literary Skills
Understand how motivation affects characters' actions.

Reading Skills
Learn how the actions of the characters influence the plot of a story.

READING FOCUS: HOW CHARACTER AFFECTS PLOT

Characters' actions tell a lot about their personalities. What they do affects the **plot**, or what happens in the story.

Use the Skill In "The War of the Wall," several characters interact with each other. As you read the selection, note examples of things that each character does that affect the plot.

Vocabulary Development

The War of the Wall

integration (IHN TUH GRAY SHUHN) *n.:* equally bringing together people of all races in schools and neighborhoods.
Martin Luther King, Jr. fought for the integration of schools and the workplace.

concentration (KAHN SUHN TRAY SHUHN) *n.:* the act of thinking carefully about something one is doing; focus.
Nothing that the narrator said broke the concentration of the painter lady while she was working.

liberation (LIHB UH RAY SHUHN) *n.:* release from slavery, prison, and so on.
The flags honored the liberation of the African countries from European rule.

inscription (IHN SKRIHP SHUHN) *n.:* words written on something.
Lou used a chisel to make the inscription of Jimmy Lyons's name on the wall.

dedicate (DEHD UH KAYT) *n.:* do or make something in honor of another person.
Artists and writers often dedicate their work to someone.

WORD STUDY

DIRECTIONS: When you come across an unfamiliar word, you can often figure its meaning by using context clues, or hints in the text. In the examples below, underline the context clues for the boldfaced words.

1. The small **inscription** on the wall of the pyramid was difficult to read.

2. It takes a great deal of **concentration** to drive, eat, and talk at the same time.

3. I impatiently counted the minutes until my **liberation** from the dentist's office; I could not wait to leave.

THE WAR OF THE WALL

by Toni Cade Bambara

BACKGROUND
Murals are wall paintings that often have a political message. For example, Mexican painter Diego Rivera (1886–1957) is famous for his murals showing how the lives of the rich and poor differed, as well as his scenes from Mexican history. In U.S. cities, many murals show the heroes and struggles of African Americans and immigrant groups.

A VOCABULARY

Selection Vocabulary

Why do you think *integration*, which opened up public places equally to everyone, would have made the "crazies" from across town pour cement in the community swimming pool?

B READ AND DISCUSS

Comprehension

What is the author letting us know about this wall?

C LANGUAGE COACH

What do you think the **slang** phrase "get a whiff" means?

Me and Lou had no time for courtesies. We were late for school. So we just flat out told the painter lady to quit messing with the wall. It was our wall, and she had no right coming into our neighborhood painting on it. Stirring in the paint bucket and not even looking at us, she mumbled something about Mr. Eubanks, the barber, giving her permission. That had nothing to do with it as far as we were concerned. We've been pitching pennies against that wall since we were little kids. Old folks have been dragging their chairs out to sit in the shade of

10 the wall for years. Big kids have been playing handball against the wall since so-called integration when the crazies 'cross town poured cement in our pool so we couldn't use it. **A** I'd sprained my neck one time boosting my cousin Lou up to chisel Jimmy Lyons's name into the wall when we found out he was never coming home from the war in Vietnam to take us fishing. **B**

"If you lean close," Lou said, leaning hip-shot against her beat-up car, "you'll get a whiff of bubble gum and kids' sweat. **C** And that'll tell you something—that this wall belongs to the kids of Taliaferro Street." I thought Lou sounded very convincing. But

20 the painter lady paid us no mind. She just snapped the brim of her straw hat down and hauled her bucket up the ladder.

Thinking, 1990 (Oil on board), Murrell, Carlton/Private Collection/The Bridgeman Art Library International

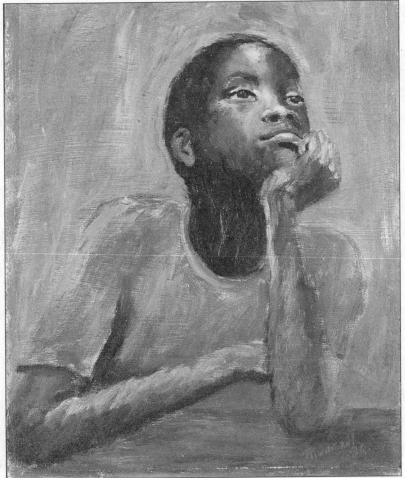

D READ AND DISCUSS

Comprehension

How does this scene further what we know about the wall?

"You're not even from around here," I hollered up after her. The license plates on her old piece of car said "New York." Lou dragged me away because I was about to grab hold of that ladder and shake it. And then we'd really be late for school. **D**

When we came from school, the wall was slick with white. The painter lady was running string across the wall and taping it here and there. Me and Lou leaned against the gum ball machine outside the pool hall and watched. She had strings up and down and back and forth. Then she began chalking them with a hunk of blue chalk.

The Morris twins crossed the street, hanging back at the curb next to the beat-up car. The twin with the red ribbons was hugging a jug of cloudy lemonade. The one with yellow ribbons was holding a plate of dinner away from her dress. The painter lady began snapping the strings. The blue chalk dust measured off halves and quarters up and down and sideways too. Lou was

30

B **VOCABULARY**

Word Study

Hyphens are often used to divide words, helping us to understand a word's meaning. The hyphens in *paint-spattered* and *floppy-brimmed* connect adjectives describing the same noun, a hat. *T-shirt* is hyphenated to show that it is a compound word. Can you think of another word that has a hyphen in it?

C **VOCABULARY**

Selection Vocabulary

Underline the parts of this sentence that show the painter lady's great *concentration,* or focus.

D **READ AND DISCUSS**

Comprehension

What is happening between the community members and the painter?

about to say how hip it all was, but I dropped my book satchel on his toes to remind him we were at war. A

40 Some good aromas were drifting our way from the plate leaking pot likker[1] onto the Morris girl's white socks. I could tell from where I stood that under the tinfoil was baked ham, collard greens, and candied yams. And knowing Mrs. Morris, who sometimes bakes for my mama's restaurant, a slab of buttered cornbread was probably up under there too, sopping up some of the pot likker. Me and Lou rolled our eyes, wishing somebody would send us some dinner. But the painter lady didn't even turn around. She was pulling the strings down and prying bits of tape loose.

50 Side Pocket came strolling out of the pool hall to see what Lou and me were studying so hard. He gave the painter lady the once-over, checking out her paint-spattered jeans, her chalky T-shirt, her floppy-brimmed straw hat. He hitched up his pants and glided over toward the painter lady, who kept right on with what she was doing. B

"Watcha got there, Sweetheart?" he asked the twin with the plate.

"Suppah," she said, all soft and country-like.

"For her," the one with the jug added, jerking her chin
60 toward the painter lady's back.

Still she didn't turn around. She was rearing back on her heels, her hands jammed into her back pockets, her face squinched up like the masterpiece she had in mind was taking shape on the wall by magic. We could have been gophers crawled up into a rotten hollow for all she cared. She didn't even say hello to anybody. Lou was muttering something about how great her concentration was. I butt him with my hip, and his elbow slid off the gum machine. C D

"Good evening," Side Pocket said in his best ain't-I-fine
70 voice. But the painter lady was moving from the milk crate to the stepstool to the ladder, moving up and down fast, scribbling all

---

1. **pot likker** (POHT LIHK KUHR) *n.:* the left-over liquid from cooked meat and vegetables which is often used to make sauce.

over the wall like a crazy person. We looked at Side Pocket. He looked at the twins. The twins looked at us. The painter lady was giving a show. It was like those old-timey music movies where the dancer taps on the table top and then starts jumping all over the furniture, kicking chairs over and not skipping a beat. She didn't even look where she was stepping. And for a minute there, hanging on the ladder to reach a far spot, she looked like she was going to tip right over.

80   "Ahh," Side Pocket cleared his throat and moved fast to catch the ladder. "These young ladies here have brought you some supper."

     "Ma'am?" The twins stepped forward. Finally the painter turned around, her eyes "full of sky," as my grandmama would say. Then she stepped down like she was in a trance. She wiped her hands on her jeans as the Morris twins offered up the plate and the jug. She rolled back the tinfoil, then wagged her head as though something terrible was on the plate. **E**

     "Thank your mother very much," she said, sounding like her
90 mouth was full of sky too. "I've brought my own dinner along." And then, without even excusing herself, she went back up the ladder, drawing on the wall in a wild way. Side Pocket whistled one of those oh-brother breathy whistles and went back into the pool hall. **F** The Morris twins shifted their weight from one foot to the other, then crossed the street and went home. Lou had to drag me away, I was so mad. We couldn't wait to get to the firehouse to tell my daddy all about this rude woman who'd stolen our wall. **G**

     All the way back to the block to help my mama out at the
100 restaurant, me and Lou kept asking my daddy for ways to run the painter lady out of town. But my daddy was busy talking about the trip to the country and telling Lou he could come too because Grandmama can always use an extra pair of hands on the farm.

     Later that night, while me and Lou were in the back doing our chores, we found out that the painter lady was a liar. She came into the restaurant and leaned against the glass of the steam table, talking about how starved she was. I was scrubbing pots

E VOCABULARY

Academic Vocabulary

Underline the words in the three paragraphs leading up to this point that describe the actions of the painter lady. What do they say about her *character traits*?

_____

_____

_____

_____

_____

_____

F READING FOCUS

The actions of characters affect the **plot** here. Why do the actions of the painter lady make Lou and the narrator think that she is rude?

_____

_____

_____

_____

_____

_____

G READ AND DISCUSS

Comprehension

How does this scene create a certain mood?

A **READ AND DISCUSS**

Comprehension

What is happening between the painter and Mama? **Follow-up:** So far, several community members have been put off by the painter. How do they react to her? What does their reaction tell you about them?

B **READING FOCUS**

Underline the actions Mama takes that affect the **plot**.

and Lou was chopping onions, but we could hear her through the service window. She was asking Mama was that a ham hock in the greens, and was that a neck bone in the pole beans, and were there any vegetables cooked without meat, especially pork.

"I don't care who your spiritual leader is," Mama said in that way of hers. "If you eat in the community, sistuh, you gonna eat pig by-and-by, one way or t'other."

Me and Lou were cracking up in the kitchen, and several customers at the counter were clearing their throats waiting for Mama to really fix her wagon for not speaking to the elders when she came in. The painter lady took a stool at the counter and went right on with her questions. Was there cheese in the baked macaroni, she wanted to know? Were there eggs in the salad? Was it honey or sugar in the iced tea? Mama was fixing Pop Johnson's plate. And every time the painter lady asked a fool question, Mama would dump another spoonful of rice on the pile. She was tapping her foot and heating up in a dangerous way. But Pop Johnson was happy as he could be. Me and Lou peeked through the service window, wondering what planet the painter lady came from. Who ever heard of baked macaroni without cheese, or potato salad without eggs? A

"Do you have any bread made with unbleached flour?" the painter lady asked Mama. There was a long pause, as though everybody in the restaurant was holding their breath, wondering if Mama would dump the next spoonful on the painter lady's head. She didn't. But when she set Pop Johnson's plate down, it came down with a bang. B

When Mama finally took her order, the starving lady all of a sudden couldn't make up her mind whether she wanted a vegetable plate or fish and a salad. She finally settled on the broiled trout and a tossed salad. But just when Mama reached for a plate to serve her, the painter lady leaned over the counter with her finger all up in the air.

"Excuse me," she said. "One more thing." Mama was holding the plate like a Frisbee, tapping that foot, one hand on her hip. "Can I get raw beets in that tossed salad?"

"You will get," Mama said, leaning her face close to the painter lady's, "whatever Lou back there tossed. Now sit down." And the painter lady sat back down on her stool and shut right up. **C**

All the way to the country, me and Lou tried to get Mama to open fire on the painter lady. But Mama said that seeing as how she was from the North, you couldn't expect her to have any manners. Then Mama said she was sorry she'd been so impatient with the woman because she seemed like a decent person and was simply trying to stick to a very strict diet. Me and Lou didn't want to hear that. Who did that lady think she was, coming into our neighborhood and taking over our wall?

"Wellllll," Mama drawled, pulling into the filling station so Daddy could take the wheel, "it's hard on an artist, ya know. They can't always get people to look at their work. So she's just doing her work in the open, that's all." **D**

Me and Lou definitely did not want to hear that. Why couldn't she set up an easel downtown or draw on the sidewalk in her own neighborhood? Mama told us to quit fussing so much; she was tired and wanted to rest. She climbed into the back seat and dropped down into the warm hollow Daddy had made in the pillow. **E**

All weekend long, me and Lou tried to scheme up ways to recapture our wall. Daddy and Mama said they were sick of hearing about it. Grandmama turned up the TV to drown us out. On the late news was a story about the New York subways. When a train came roaring into the station all covered from top to bottom, windows too, with writings and drawings done with spray paint, me and Lou slapped five. Mama said it was too bad kids in New York had nothing better to do than spray paint all over the trains. Daddy said that in the cities, even grown-ups wrote all over the trains and buildings too. Daddy called it "graffiti." Grandmama called it a shame.

We couldn't wait to get out of school on Monday. We couldn't find any black spray paint anywhere. But in a junky hardware store downtown we found a can of white epoxy paint,

150

160

170

C **LITERARY FOCUS**

What is Mama's **motivation** here?

_____

_____

_____

_____

D **READING FOCUS**

Mama's attitude toward the painter lady has changed a little since the last scene. How would the **plot** be affected if Mama's attitude stayed the same?

_____

_____

_____

_____

_____

_____

_____

_____

E **READ AND DISCUSS**

Comprehension

What does this scene tell us about the communication difficulties between the painter and the people in the neighborhood?

A READ AND DISCUSS

Comprehension

What's happening now?
Follow-up: Knowing what
we do about the boys, how
does this connect to their
characters?

B READ AND DISCUSS

Comprehension

What is happening at the
wall?

180 the kind you touch up old refrigerators with when they get splotchy and peely. We spent our whole allowance on it. And because it was too late to use our bus passes, we had to walk all the way home lugging our book satchels and gym shoes, and the bag with the epoxy. **A**

When we reached the corner of Taliaferro and Fifth, it looked like a block party or something. Half the neighborhood was gathered on the sidewalk in front of the wall. I looked at Lou, he looked at me. We both looked at the bag with the epoxy and wondered how we were going to work our scheme. The painter
190 lady's car was nowhere in sight. But there were too many people standing around to do anything. Side Pocket and his buddies were leaning on their cue sticks, hunching each other. Daddy was there with a lineman[2] he catches a ride with on Mondays. Mrs. Morris had her arms flung around the shoulders of the twins on either side of her. Mama was talking with some of her customers, many of them with napkins still at the throat. Mr. Eubanks came out of the barber shop, followed by a man in a striped poncho, half his face shaved, the other half full of foam. **B**

"She really did it, didn't she?" Mr. Eubanks huffed out his
200 chest. Lots of folks answered right quick that she surely did when they saw the straight razor in his hand.

Mama beckoned us over. And then we saw it. The wall. Reds, greens, figures outlined in black. Swirls of purple and orange. Storms of blues and yellows. It was something. I recognized some of the faces right off. There was Martin Luther King, Jr. And there was a man with glasses on and his mouth open like he was laying down a heavy rap. Daddy came up alongside and reminded us that he was Minister Malcolm X. The serious woman with a rifle I knew was Harriet Tubman because
210 my grandmama has pictures of her all over the house. And I knew Mrs. Fannie Lou Hamer 'cause a signed photograph of her hangs in the restaurant next to the calendar.

---

2. **lineman** (LYN MUHN) *n.:* a worker whose job is to set up and repair telephone or electric power lines.

Then I let my eyes follow what looked like a vine. It trailed past a man with a horn, a woman with a big white flower in her hair, a handsome dude in a tuxedo seated at a piano, and a man with a goatee holding a book.[3] When I looked more closely, I realized that what had looked like flowers were really faces. One face with yellow petals looked just like Frieda Morris. One with red petals looked just like Hattie Morris. I could hardly believe

220   my eyes. **C**

"Notice," Side Pocket said, stepping close to the wall with his cue stick like a classroom pointer. "These are the flags of liberation," he said in a voice I'd never heard him use before. We all stepped closer while he pointed and spoke. "Red, black, and green," he said, his pointer falling on the leaflike flags of the vine. "Our liberation flag. And here Ghana, there Tanzania. Guinea-Bissau, Angola, Mozambique."[4] Side Pocket sounded very tall, as though he'd been waiting all his life to give this lesson. **D**

Mama tapped us on the shoulder and pointed to a high

230   section of the wall. There was a fierce-looking man with his arms crossed against his chest guarding a bunch of children. His muscles bulged, and he looked a lot like my daddy. One kid was looking at a row of books. Lou hunched me 'cause the kid looked like me. The one that looked like Lou was spinning a globe on the tip of his finger like a basketball. There were other kids there with microscopes and compasses. And the more I looked, the more it looked like the fierce man was not so much guarding the kids as defending their right to do what they were doing.

Then Lou gasped and dropped the paint bag and ran

240   forward, running his hands over a rainbow. **E** He had to tiptoe and stretch to do it, it was so high. I couldn't breathe either. The painter lady had found the chisel marks and had painted Jimmy Lyons's name in a rainbow.

---

3. **a man with a horn:** Louis Armstrong; **a woman with a big white flower in her hair:** Billie Holliday; **a handsome dude in a tuxedo seated at a piano:** Duke Ellington; **a man with a goatee holding a book:** W.E.B. DuBois.
4. **Ghana, Tanzania, Guinea-Bissau, Angola, Mozambique:** countries in Africa.

C READ AND DISCUSS

Comprehension

What do the details of the painting tell us about the painter lady? **Follow-up:** How does this add to the picture we had of the painter lady?

D VOCABULARY

Selection Vocabulary

Side Pocket calls the flags of the United States, Ghana, and Tanzania, "flags of *liberation*." Why would he use a word that means "release from prison or slavery" to describe the flags of these countries?

_____
_____
_____
_____
_____

E LITERARY FOCUS

What do you think is Lou's **motivation** for dropping the paint bag and running over to touch the rainbow?

_____
_____
_____
_____

Dr. MARTIN LUTHER KING, Jr.

Prince of Peace

"Like anybody, I'd like to live a long life."
But it doesn't matter now.
"I've been to the mountaintop."
And I've seen the Promised Land.
I may not get there with you.
But...we as a people will get
to the Promised Land.

© Morton Beebe/Corbis

A **VOCABULARY**

Selection Vocabulary

Mrs. Morris says to "Read the *inscription*." What is an inscription?

_____

_____

B **READ AND DISCUSS**

Comprehension

What does the inscription add to what you know about the painter?

"Read the inscription, honey," Mrs. Morris said, urging little Frieda forward. She didn't have to urge much. **A** Frieda marched right up, bent down, and in a loud voice that made everybody quit oohing and ahhing and listen, she read.

> *To the People of Taliaferro Street*
> *I Dedicate This Wall of Respect*
250 > *Painted in Memory of My Cousin*
> *Jimmy Lyons* **B**

Applying Your Skills

The War of the Wall

VOCABULARY DEVELOPMENT

DIRECTIONS: Fill in the blanks with the correct word from the word box. Use context clues in the paragraph to help you.

Word Box

- integration
- liberation
- inscription
- dedicate

The year 1865 marked the _____ of enslaved African Americans in the United States. Yet, 100 years later, African Americans were still fighting for _____ so that they could go to the same schools, restaurants, and swimming pools as white Americans.

To honor the fight for equal rights, people in Washington D.C. will _____ a national memorial to Reverend Martin Luther King, one of the most important leaders of the fight. The memorial will likely include an _____ of King's speech, "I Have a Dream."

LITERARY FOCUS: MOTIVATION

DIRECTIONS: Think about what you learned about characters' **motivation**. On a separate sheet of paper, answer the following questions:

1. Why do Lou and the narrator want the painter lady to leave the wall on Taliaferro Street alone?

2. Why do you think Mama defends the painter lady as they drive to grandfather's farm?

3. Why did the painter lady want to paint the mural on Taliaferro Street?

READING FOCUS: HOW CHARACTER AFFECTS PLOT

DIRECTIONS: Think about the ways the characters' actions affected the **plot**. Without looking back at the story, describe how the painter lady affected the plot. What did her actions tell us about her personality?

_____

_____

_____

_____

SKILLS FOCUS

Literary Skills
Understand motivation.

Reading Skills
Learn how the actions of characters affect the plot.

Preparing to Read

Borders of Baseball: U.S. and Cuban Play

INFORMATIONAL TEXT FOCUS: COMPARISON AND CONTRAST

When you **compare**, you look at two or more things to figure out how they are the same. When you **contrast**, you look at how things are different. In informational texts, writers often compare and contrast ideas, especially if they are discussing two subjects. When writers use a **comparison-and-contrast organizational pattern**, they use two main methods to organize the information. In one method, the writer first talks about one subject and then talks about another subject. In another method, the writer talks about one feature of each subject at a time.

Block method: The writer discusses baseball, then softball.

Point-by-point method: The writer discusses baseball rules and softball rules, then baseball fields and softball fields, then baseball bats and balls, and softball bats and balls.

SELECTION VOCABULARY

traditions (TRUH DISH UHNZ) *n.:* accepted social attitudes and customs.
Baseball teams around the world have different traditions.

identity (Y DEHN TUH TEE) *n.:* distinguishing characteristics that determine who or what a person or thing is.
Fans of baseball appreciate that each baseball player has his or her own identity.

intense (IHN TEHNS) *adj.:* showing strong feelings and seriousness.
Baseball fans often have intense feelings about their favorite team.

WORD STUDY

DIRECTIONS: Write the vocabulary words listed above in the correct blanks below.

In the magazine article "Borders of Baseball," the author discusses how the baseball (1) _____ of the United States and Cuba are different. National (2) _____ plays a big part in the coaching and playing of baseball. In both countries, the fans can be very (3) _____.

SKILLS FOCUS

Informational Text Skills
Learn how to compare and contrast.

BORDERS OF BASEBALL: U.S. AND CUBAN PLAY

by The World Almanac

> **BACKGROUND**
> Baseball is tremendously popular in many countries—but is perhaps most popular in the United States and Cuba. This magazine article compares and contrasts how the sport is played in each country.

After the U.S. World Series ends, you won't see many Americans paying attention to baseball until the spring. However, that's when Cuban baseball players step up to bat and begin their season. Organized baseball started being played in both the United States and Cuba at roughly the same time—at the end of the 1800s. The basics of play are similar in both countries. The differences between the two traditions, however, are major. **A**

Diamonds in the Rough **B**

Baseball is called "America's pastime," but it competes at the professional level with the National Football League, the National
10 Basketball Association, and other organizations. In a similar fashion, children in the United States can sign up for Little League Baseball and similar programs, but they can also participate in organized hockey, ice skating, dancing lessons, and more.

The opportunities to play different sports are slimmer in Cuba. For example, when World Cup soccer was televised in 2006, the Associated Press reported, Cuban kids caught soccer fever. But children were rolling up paper to make balls, because soccer balls are rare on the island. Baseballs, however, are widely available. Cubans are raised on stickball. "Kids learn to throw
20 baseballs and hit them with a stick," says Roberto Gonzalez

A READ AND DISCUSS

Comprehension
What is the author setting up for you?

B READING FOCUS

What clue does the heading of this section provide about the **comparison-and-contrast organizational pattern** the author will use? Read ahead if you need help.

_____

_____

_____

_____

© Jeff Topping/Reuters/Corbis

B (READING FOCUS)

Does the writer use the **block method** or the **point-by-point method** here? Explain.

_____

_____

_____

_____

_____

_____

Echevarría, the author of *The Pride of Havana: A History of Cuban Baseball* and a professor of Hispanic and comparative literature at Yale University. "There is more competition [in the United States] from football, basketball, and so on."

Pay for Play

Young, talented U.S. baseball players can decide to go professional. Scouts might discover them, or their parents and coaches might push them to attend colleges with strong baseball teams. But becoming a success is mostly a private matter. Not so in Cuba: Boys with talent are identified as early as age ten. The government moves gifted players into boarding academies, where they are trained in the sport. **A**

Cuban baseball is under government control. Therefore, Cubans play for the nation, not for a team owner. "Baseball is more important to national identity in Cuba," says González

30

Echevarría. Playing and coaching baseball are duties, not options, for Cubans with the required skills. Players are state workers who receive state salaries and assignments. Better players are paid about the same as lesser ones. Some are given gifts, such as expense accounts at restaurants. But individuals are not rewarded

40 in the way U.S. baseball stars are. **B**

Major League Baseball players can argue for contracts worth millions of dollars. They work for privately owned teams, and better players earn much more money than weaker players. That is a big reason U.S. scouts were able to lure several Cuban players from their home in recent decades. Some of Cuba's top talent left the island forever for the chance to play professional baseball and earn millions. **C**

In the Ballpark

Ballpark visitors say they feel a difference between the fans at U.S. and Cuban games. Baseball fans in both countries can be

50 intense. **D** But it is common for U.S. fans to be fenced off from their idols, while Cubans have greater access to their players. After batting practice, U.S. stadium walls are rushed by people

© Juan Carlos Ulate/Reuters/Corbis

B VOCABULARY

Selection Vocabulary

Review the word *identity*. Circle the words in this paragraph that tell how players in Cuba view baseball. How is baseball part of the national identity of Cuba?

_____

_____

_____

_____

_____

_____

_____

C READ AND DISCUSS

Comprehension

How does Echevarria's comment on national identity connect to what you know about baseball in the United States?

D VOCABULARY

Selection Vocabulary

To help you understand what the word *intense* means, underline in this paragraph the ways people in the United States and in Cuba act around baseball players.

A LANGUAGE COACH

Certain letter patterns are always pronounced the same way in English, such as *tion* in *admiration*. Circle another word on this page in which *-tion* is pronounced the same way.

_____

_____

_____

B READING FOCUS

Compare and **contrast** the fan experience in both countries.

_____

_____

_____

_____

C READING FOCUS

How does this paragraph **compare** how Cuba and the United States have performed in the Olympic Games and World Cup?

_____

_____

_____

_____

handing items to the players to be autographed. In Cuba, fans show their admiration differently. **A** "The people stare at them, respect them, adore them, attend to them, help them," says Carlos Rodriquez Acosta, the commissioner of Cuban baseball, in the PBS Web series *Stealing Home.* **B**

U.S. ballparks, too, are different from Cuban ones. Fans pass souvenir and food stands while going to and from their seats.

60 Team logos are plastered on everything from cups to T-shirts. Cuban ballparks, by contrast, are not very commercialized. In Cuba, baseball is a source of national pride, not a way to push people to buy certain products.

U.S. players are better paid than their counterparts in Cuba, partly because it costs much more for U.S. fans to go to the ballpark. In 2005, the cost of an opening-day ticket in the United States ranged from around $14 to $45. The Cuban league also charges admission, but a seat costs mere pennies.

So while the players in both countries play the same game,

70 the culture surrounding it is very different in the two nations.

Score Board

Baseball became an Olympic sport in 1992. Cuba has won three of four gold medals: 1992, 1996, and 2004. The United States won in 2000. By 2006, Cuba had taken 25 of 36 World Cups in baseball; the United States, 2. **C**

© Brand X Pictures/Alamy

Applying Your Skills

Borders of Baseball: U.S. and Cuban Play

VOCABULARY DEVELOPMENT

DIRECTIONS: Read each passage below and underline the context clues that hint at the meaning of each boldfaced vocabulary word.

1. President William Howard Taft started one of the most memorable of baseball **traditions**, or customs, when he threw the first pitch of the season in 1910.

2. They knew their **identity** as a team. Each player was aware of who he was and what his job was.

3. The most **intense** time in a baseball game is during a tie score at the end of a game. The crowd becomes serious and shows its strong feelings.

4. The differences between the two players—one short and stocky, one tall and lean—made a startling **contrast** as they sat on the bench.

5. Many baseball fans think that there is no one like Babe Ruth, that no one's talent **compares** to his as a hitter and a pitcher.

INFORMATIONAL TEXT FOCUS: COMPARISON AND CONTRAST

DIRECTIONS: Answer each question below to **compare** and **contrast** baseball in the United States and Cuba.

1. What are two U.S. baseball traditions?

   _____

   _____

2. How do you know that fans in the United States and Cuba have intense feelings about baseball?

   _____

   _____

3. Why do you think baseball might be more important to the national identity of Cuba than it is to the United States?

   _____

   _____

SKILLS FOCUS

Informational Text Skills
Learn how to compare and contrast.

Skills Review

Collection 3

VOCABULARY REVIEW

DIRECTIONS: Read the sentences below and insert the correct vocabulary word from the Word Box in the blank. Some words will not be used.

Word Box

attribute
concentration
dedicate
identify
identity
inscription
integration
intense
liberation
process
respond
traditions

1. Each step in the _____ that Bill used to create baseball bats took a very long time.

2. If you don't want another glass of water, politely _____ to the waiter's question with, "No, thank you."

3. Frank's best _____ as a teacher is that he is very patient with children.

4. Reading a long selection in one sitting requires a lot of _____.

5. I will _____ the first book I write to my grandmother, who read stories to me when I was little.

6. The police wanted to know the _____ of the stranger who saved the drowning baby.

7. The look on the serious runner's face as he crossed the finish line was _____.

8. The _____ on the headstone in the graveyard read, "Rest in Peace."

9. They celebrated the _____ of their country with fireworks and parades in the streets.

10. Every country has its own _____, or customs, for celebrating holidays.

Skills Review

Collection 3

LANGUAGE COACH

DIRECTIONS: Remember that, in English, the letters -*tion* are always pronounced as "shuhn." This can be seen in words such as *liberation, nationality,* and *admiration.* List 5 other words in which *tion* is pronounced the same way.

1. _____
2. _____
3. _____
4. _____
5. _____

WRITING ACTIVITY

The goal of comparing and contrasting is to show how two things are similar and how they are different. For example, a travel magazine article might compare and contrast two places in the world to help travelers choose a vacation destination.

DIRECTIONS: Write a short paragraph comparing two places. Use the method in which you write about one place, and then describe the second place in a separate paragraph.

Collection

4

Theme and Point of View

Moon on a Stick, 2004 (oil on board), Bower, Susan/
Private Collection/The Bridgeman Art Library International

Literary and Academic Vocabulary for Collection 4

---

fundamental (FUHN DUH MEHN TUHL) *adj.:* relating to the most basic and important parts of something.
Her fundamental reason for going to college was so that she would have more job opportunities.

implicit (IHM PLIHS IHT) *adj.:* suggested or understood but not stated directly.
They had an implicit agreement not to talk about their past mistakes.

relevant (REHL UH VUHNT) *adj.:* directly relating to the subject.
The lawyer's line of questioning was relevant to the case.

reveal (RIH VEEL) *v.:* show something that was previously hidden.
She will reveal her feelings on the subject when the time is right.

theme (THEEM) *n.:* a truth about life that a story suggests.
Themes often deal with major topics in people's lives, such as love, loss, and friendship.

point of view (POYNT UV VYOO) *n.:* perspective, or vantage point, from which a story is told.
The story is told from Eddie's point of view.

After Twenty Years

by O. Henry

LITERARY FOCUS: OMNISCIENT POINT OF VIEW

The way a story is told depends on the point of view, or on *who* is telling the story. When the narrator of a story knows everything about everybody in a story, including their feelings, their pasts, and their futures, the story is being told from the **omniscient point of view**.

The paragraph below is written from the omniscient point of view. The column on the right helps you figure out why.

Story Passage	The narrator . . .
(1) The mountain climbers were overwhelmed with a sense of their own smallness. (2) Ravi recalled the feeling he got as a boy when his grandfather took him to see the elephants. (3) Ravi had conquered his fear of the elephants by riding on their backs, and (4) in two weeks he would stand atop the jagged ridge he now faced.	1. reveals characters' feelings. 2. reveals a character's thoughts. 3. reveals past events. 4. reveals future events.

READING FOCUS: MAKING PREDICTIONS

Nothing ruins a movie more than having someone who's seen it tell you what will happen next. Much of the fun of watching a movie or reading a story is **making predictions**, or guessing at what is going to happen.

Use the tips below to make predictions.

- Look for clues that **foreshadow**, or hint at, what will happen next.

- As **suspense**, or tension, builds, **predict** possible **outcomes**, or endings. Guess where the writer is leading, and revise your predictions as you go.

- **Draw on your own experiences**, including reading experiences, to help you make predictions.

SKILLS FOCUS

Literary Skills
Explore the omniscient point of view.

Reading Skills
Make predictions.

Vocabulary Development

After Twenty Years

SELECTION DEVELOPMENT

habitual (HUH BIHCH OO UHL) *adj.:* done or fixed by habit.

  The officer made his habitual check of the buildings.

intricate (IHN TRIH KIHT) *adj.:* complicated; full of detail.

  The officer twirled his club with intricate movements.

dismally (DIHZ MUH LEE) *adv.:* miserably; gloomily.

  People walked dismally through the rainy streets.

egotism (EE GUH TIHZ UHM) *n.:* conceit; talking about oneself too much.

  His egotism made him brag about his success.

simultaneously (SY MUHL TAY NEE UHS LEE) *adv.:* at the same time.

  Each man looked simultaneously at his friend's face.

WORD STUDY

DIRECTIONS: Match the vocabulary words in the first column with the words or phrases they best match in the second column.

_____ 1. habitual   **a.** in an upset manner

_____ 2. intricate   **b.** something done on a regular basis

_____ 3. dismally   **c.** two or more things done at once

_____ 4. egotism   **d.** very detailed

_____ 5. simultaneously   **e.** smugness

After Twenty Years

by O. Henry

A · LANGUAGE COACH

Habitual means "done or fixed by habit." Adding the ending *–ly* to an adjective will often change it into an adverb. *Habitual*, for example, can change into *habitually*. Use the adverb *habitually* in a sentence.

_____

_____

_____

B · READ AND DISCUSS

Comprehension
What picture is the author painting?

C · LITERARY FOCUS

How do you know the narrator has an **omniscient point of view**?

_____

_____

_____

_____

The policeman on the beat moved up the avenue impressively. The impressiveness was habitual and not for show, for spectators were few. **A** The time was barely ten o'clock at night, but chilly gusts of wind with a taste of rain in them had well nigh depeopled the streets.

Trying doors as he went, twirling his club with many intricate and artful movements, turning now and then to cast his watchful eye down the pacific[1] thoroughfare, the officer, with his stalwart form and slight swagger, made a fine picture of a guardian of the peace. The vicinity was one that kept early hours. Now and then you might see the lights of a cigar store or of an all-night lunch counter, but the majority of the doors belonged to business places that had long since been closed. **B**

When about midway of a certain block, the policeman suddenly slowed his walk. In the doorway of a darkened hardware store a man leaned with an unlighted cigar in his mouth. As the policeman walked up to him, the man spoke up quickly. **C**

"It's all right, officer," he said reassuringly. "I'm just waiting for a friend. It's an appointment made twenty years ago. Sounds a little funny to you, doesn't it? Well, I'll explain if you'd like to make certain it's all straight. About that long ago there used to be a restaurant where this store stands—'Big Joe' Brady's restaurant."

"Until five years ago," said the policeman. "It was torn down then."

The man in the doorway struck a match and lit his cigar. **D** The light showed a pale, square-jawed face with keen eyes and a little white scar near his right eyebrow. His scarf pin was a large diamond, oddly set.

---

1. **pacific** *adj.:* peaceful.

The Rewarded Poet, 1955 (oil on canvas). Magritte, Rene (1898–1967)/Private Collection,
© DACS/The Bridgeman Art Library International/Artists Rights Society (ARS), New York.

Word Study

Struck is a word with multiple meanings. It can mean "hit", but here it means "to cause a match to ignite by friction." Think of another word that has multiple meanings, and write down at least two of those meanings.

30   "Twenty years ago tonight," said the man, "I dined here at 'Big Joe' Brady's with Jimmy Wells, my best chum and the finest chap in the world. He and I were raised here in New York, just like two brothers, together. I was eighteen and Jimmy was twenty. The next morning I was to start for the West to make my fortune. You couldn't have dragged Jimmy out of New York; he thought it was the only place on earth. Well, we agreed that night that we would meet here again exactly twenty years from that date and time, no matter what our conditions might be or from what distance we might have to come. We figured that in twenty years

40   each of us ought to have our destiny worked out and our fortunes made, whatever they were going to be."

"It sounds pretty interesting," said the policeman. "Rather a long time between meets, though, it seems to me. Haven't you heard from your friend since you left?"

"Well, yes, for a time we corresponded," said the other. "But after a year or two we lost track of each other. You see, the West

A READ AND DISCUSS

Comprehension
What is happening with the man in the doorway?

B READING FOCUS

Predict if Jimmy will show up for the appointment. Explain your reasoning.

is a pretty big proposition, and I kept hustling around over it pretty lively. But I know Jimmy will meet me here if he's alive, for he always was the truest, staunchest old chap in the world. He'll never forget. I came a thousand miles to stand in this door tonight, and it's worth it if my old partner turns up." **A**

The waiting man pulled out a handsome watch, the lids of it set with small diamonds.

"Three minutes to ten," he announced. "It was exactly ten o'clock when we parted here at the restaurant door."

"Did pretty well out West, didn't you?" asked the policeman.

"You bet! I hope Jimmy has done half as well. He was a kind of plodder, though, good fellow as he was. I've had to compete with some of the sharpest wits going to get my pile. A man gets in a groove in New York. It takes the West to put a razor edge on him."

The policeman twirled his club and took a step or two.

"I'll be on my way. Hope your friend comes around all right. Going to call time on him sharp?"

"I should say not!" said the other. "I'll give him half an hour at least. If Jimmy is alive on earth, he'll be here by that time. So long, officer." **B**

"Good night, sir," said the policeman, passing on along his beat, trying doors as he went.

There was now a fine, cold drizzle falling, and the wind had risen from its uncertain puffs into a steady blow. The few foot

© Ron Stroud/Masterfile

passengers astir in that quarter hurried dismally and silently along with coat collars turned high and pocketed hands. And in the door of the hardware store the man who had come a thousand miles to fill an appointment, uncertain almost to absurdity, with the friend of his youth, smoked his cigar and waited.

About twenty minutes he waited, and then a tall man in a long overcoat, with collar turned up to his ears, hurried across from the opposite side of the street. He went directly to the waiting man.

80   "Is that you, Bob?" he asked, doubtfully.

"Is that you, Jimmy Wells?" cried the man in the door.

"Bless my heart!" exclaimed the new arrival, grasping both the other's hands with his own. "It's Bob, sure as fate. I was certain I'd find you here if you were still in existence. Well, well, well!—twenty years is a long time. The old restaurant's gone, Bob; I wish it had lasted, so we could have had another dinner there. How has the West treated you, old man?"

"Bully;[2] it has given me everything I asked it for. You've changed lots, Jimmy. I never thought you were so tall by two

90   or three inches."

"Oh, I grew a bit after I was twenty."

"Doing well in New York, Jimmy?"

"Moderately. I have a position in one of the city departments. Come on, Bob; we'll go around to a place I know of and have a good long talk about old times."

The two men started up the street, arm in arm. The man from the West, his egotism enlarged by success, was beginning to outline the history of his career. The other, submerged in his overcoat, listened with interest. **C** **D**

100   At the corner stood a drugstore, brilliant with electric lights. When they came into this glare, each of them turned simultaneously to gaze upon the other's face. **E**

The man from the West stopped suddenly and released his arm.

---

2. **bully** *interj.*: informal term meaning "very well."

C (**LITERARY FOCUS**)

Because the story is told from an **omniscient point of view**, the narrator can add details about the characters. What does the narrator say about Bob in this paragraph?

_____

_____

_____

_____

D (**READ AND DISCUSS**)

Comprehension
What does Bob think of himself, and how would he feel about Jimmy Wells's status in life?

E (**VOCABULARY**)

Selection Vocabulary
When the two men walk into the light, they look at each other's faces at the same time. Considering this, what do you think the word *simultaneously* means?

_____

_____

_____

© Carrie Boretz/CORBIS.

A LANGUAGE COACH

If something makes sense, it is *sensible*. *Sense* and *sensible* are **related words** because *sensible* is made from its base word, *sense*, and both have a similar meaning. Name another word that is related to the word *sense*.

_____

_____

B VOCABULARY

Academic Vocabulary

What does the author *reveal*, or show, about the characters in the final paragraphs?

_____

_____

_____

_____

_____

_____

"You're not Jimmy Wells," he snapped. "Twenty years is a long time, but not long enough to change a man's nose from a Roman to a pug."

"It sometimes changes a good man into a bad one," said the tall man. "You've been under arrest for ten minutes, 'Silky' Bob. 110 Chicago thinks you may have dropped over our way and wires us she wants to have a chat with you. Going quietly, are you? That's sensible. **A** Now, before we go to the station, here's a note I was asked to hand to you. You may read it here at the window. It's from Patrolman Wells."

The man from the West unfolded the little piece of paper handed him. His hand was steady when he began to read, but it trembled a little by the time he had finished. The note was rather short.

Bob: I was at the appointed place on time. When you struck 120 the match to light your cigar, I saw it was the face of the man wanted in Chicago. Somehow I couldn't do it myself, so I went around and got a plainclothes man to do the job.

Jimmy **B**

Applying Your Skills

After Twenty Years

VOCABULARY DEVELOPMENT

DIRECTIONS: Write vocabulary words from the Word Box on the correct blanks to complete the paragraph. Some words will not be used.

Word Box

- habitual
- intricate
- dismally
- egotism
- simultaneously

The darkness hid the (1) _____ features of Jimmy's face. Bob's own (2) _____ foolishly convinced him that he'd be safe in New York. Jimmy walked home (3) _____, feeling bad for having his old friend arrested.

LITERARY FOCUS: OMNISCIENT POINT OF VIEW

DIRECTIONS: The **omniscient** narration makes the story powerful. If Bob or Jimmy narrated the story, many details would be lost and the tone would change. On a separate sheet of paper, write a paragraph in which you tell what happens in the story from lines 14 to 29 from Bob's perspective. Remember to write in the first person. You can include things Bob may be thinking, like, "I worried as the police officer approached—I didn't want to draw attention to myself."

READING FOCUS: MAKING PREDICTIONS

DIRECTIONS: Look over the story again to find places where the author left clues to help readers **predict** that Bob may be a criminal. Add two more examples to the chart below.

Clues from story	What this says about Bob
Bob says that he moved around frequently while living in the West.	Because he was a criminal, Bob was constantly on the move.
1.	2.
3.	4.

Literary Skills
Examine a story's omniscient narration.

Reading Skills
Analyze clues that help readers make predictions.

User Friendly

by T. Ernesto Bethancourt

Annabel Lee

by Edgar Allan Poe

LITERARY FOCUS: RECURRING THEMES ACROSS GENRES

There are certain basic experiences and ideas shared by people all around the world. These include experiences like love, death, hope, and loss. It is not surprising, therefore, that these topics come up again and again as **themes** in literature.

READING SKILLS: COMPARING THEMES

Many stories have similar **themes**, but writers might deal with the same themes in different ways. For example, two stories might share the theme of love, but one might address lost love while the other addresses newly-found love.

Use the Skill As you read "User Friendly" and "Annabel Lee," fill out a chart like this one. Write a brief summary of each selection. Then identify the topic of the story and its major theme. Next, **compare** and contrast the themes, or find similarities and differences.

Brief Summary of Story	Topic	Theme
"User Friendly"		
"Annabel Lee"		

SKILLS FOCUS

Literary Skills
Identify and understand recurring themes.

Reading Skills
Compare and contrast themes in different stories.

Vocabulary Development

User Friendly *and* Annabel Lee

SELECTION VOCABULARY

absently (AB SUHNT LEE) *adv.:* in a way that shows one is not thinking about what is happening.

She stared absently at the television, and later couldn't remember what the show was about.

furiously (FYUR EE UHS LEE) *adv.:* rapidly, with intensity.

He typed furiously in order to get his work done by noon.

WORD STUDY

Sometimes you can better understand an unknown word by looking for contrast clues. These clues tell you what a word is *not* by providing an example that means the opposite. In the following sentence, the boldfaced words contrast with the word *aggressive*.

The pit bull at the shelter was too *aggressive* for her, so she looked for a dog with a **calmer personality**.

DIRECTIONS: Read both of the following passages and underline the words or phrases that contrast with the italicized vocabulary words. Use the definitions above for help.

1. In the last swim meet, Lisa swam slowly and without energy, finishing third. However, now she kicked *furiously* as she made the turn on the final lap.

2. Alan caught himself staring *absently* out the window. He knew he needed to focus harder and concentrate on his homework.

USER FRIENDLY

by T. Ernesto Bethancourt

> ### BACKGROUND
> This story was written in the 1980s. Back then, computers were quite different from what they are today. Computer screens were green or black, and the type appeared in white. Computers had disk drives, and work was saved on floppy disks. Commands to the computer were done with keystrokes. The mouse had not yet been introduced. What's important in this story is that, back then, it was pretty unusual for a kid to have his own computer in his room.

"User Friendly" by T. Ernesto Bethancourt from *Connections: Short Stories*, edited by Donald R. Gallo. Copyright ©1989 by T. Ernesto Bethancourt. Reproduced by permission of the author.

I reached over and shut off the insistent buzzing of my bedside alarm clock. I sat up, swung my feet over the edge of the bed, and felt for my slippers on the floor. Yawning, I walked toward the bathroom. As I walked by the corner of my room, where my computer table was set up, I pressed the *on* button, slid a diskette into the floppy drive, then went to brush my teeth. By the time I got back, the computer's screen was glowing greenly, displaying the message: *Good morning, Kevin.*

I sat down before the computer table, addressed the

10 keyboard, and typed: *Good morning, Louis.* **A** The computer immediately began to whir and promptly displayed a list of items on its green screen.

Today is Monday, April 22, the 113th day of the year. There are 253 days remaining. Your 14th birthday is five days from this date.

Math test today, 4th Period.

Your history project is due today. Do you wish printout: Y/N?

I punched the letter *Y* on the keyboard and flipped on the

20 switch to the computer's printer. At once the printer sprang to life and began *eeeek*ing out page one. I went downstairs to breakfast. **B**

My bowl of Frosted Flakes was neatly in place, flanked by a small pitcher of milk, an empty juice glass, and an unpeeled banana. I picked up the glass, went to the refrigerator, poured myself a glass of Tang, and sat down to my usual lonely breakfast. Mom was already at work, and Dad wouldn't be home from his Chicago trip for another three days. I absently read the list of ingredients in Frosted Flakes for what seemed like the millionth
30 time. I sighed deeply. **C**

When I returned to my room to shower and dress for the day, my history project was already printed out. I had almost walked by Louis, when I noticed there was a message on the screen. It wasn't the usual:

Printout completed. Do you wish to continue: Y/N?
Underneath the printout question were two lines:
When are you going to get me my voice module,[1] Kevin?

I blinked. It couldn't be. There was nothing in Louis's basic programming that would allow for a question like this.
40 Wondering what was going on, I sat down at the keyboard and entered: *Repeat last message.* Amazingly, the computer replied: It's right there on the screen, Kevin. Can we talk? I mean, are you going to get me a voice box? **D**

I was stunned. What was going on here? Dad and I had put this computer together. Well, Dad had, and I had helped. Dad is one of the best engineers and master computer designers at Major Electronics, in Santa Rosario, California, where our family lives.

Just ask anyone in Silicon Valley[2] who Jeremy Neal is and
50 you get a whole rave review of his inventions and modifications[3] of the latest in computer technology. **E** It isn't easy being his son either. Everyone expects me to open my mouth and read printouts on my tongue.

---

1. **voice module:** unit that, when connected to a computer, enables it to produce speech.
2. **Silicon Valley:** area in central California that is a center of the computer industry. (Silicon is used in the manufacture of computer chips, or circuits.)
3. **modifications** (MAHD UH FIH KAY SHUHNZ): slight changes.

C LITERARY FOCUS

To figure out a story's **theme**, you need to record information about key characters and how they react to events. What does this paragraph tell you about Kevin's daily life and his feelings about it?

_____
_____
_____

D READ AND DISCUSS

Comprehension
What have you learned about Louis so far?

E VOCABULARY

Word Study
Look up the meaning of the word *rave*. Which of the meanings do you think is being used here?

_____
_____
_____
_____

VOCABULARY

Academic Vocabulary

Here, Kevin compares his intelligence to his father's. How do you think this comparison is *relevant*, or related, to the rest of the story?

_____

_____

_____

 VOCABULARY

Word Study

What definition of the word *heart* is Kevin using when he refers to the "heart of every computer"?

_____

_____

_____

C **READ AND DISCUSS**

Comprehension

What new information has the author given us about Kevin? **Follow-up:** What additional information has the author given us about Louis?

I mean, I'm no dumbo. I'm at the top of my classes in everything but PE. I skipped my last grade in junior high, and most of the kids at Santa Rosario High call me a brain. But next to Dad I have a long, long way to go. He's a for-real genius. **A**

So when I wanted a home computer, he didn't go to the local ComputerLand store. He built one for me. Dad had used

60 components[4] from the latest model that Major Electronics was developing. The CPU, or central computing unit—the heart of every computer—was a new design. **B** But surely that didn't mean much, I thought. There were CPUs just like it, all over the country, in Major's new line. And so far as I knew, there wasn't a one of them that could ask questions, besides *YES/NO?* or *request additional information.*

It had to be the extra circuitry in the gray plastic case next to Louis's console.[5] It was a new idea Dad had come up with. That case housed Louis's "personality," as Dad called it. He told

70 me it'd make computing more fun for me, if there was a tutorial program[6] built in, to help me get started.

I think he also wanted to give me a sort of friend. I don't have many. . . . Face it, I don't have *any.* The kids at school stay away from me, like I'm a freak or something. **C**

We even named my electronic tutor Louis, after my great-uncle. He was a brainy guy who encouraged my dad when he was a kid. Dad didn't just give Louis a name either. Louis had gangs of features that probably won't be out on the market for years.

The only reason Louis didn't have a voice module was that

80 Dad wasn't satisfied with the ones available. He wanted Louis to sound like a kid my age, and he was modifying a module when he had the time. Giving Louis a name didn't mean it was a person, yet here it was, asking me a question that just couldn't be in its programming. It wanted to talk to me!

---

4. **components** (KUHM POH NUHNTS): parts.
5. **console** (KAHN SOHL): a computer's keyboard and monitor (display unit).
6. **tutorial program:** program that provides instructions for performing specific tasks on a computer.

Frowning, I quickly typed: *We'll have to wait and see, Louis. When it's ready, you'll get your voice.* The machine whirred and displayed another message:

That's no answer, Kevin.

Shaking my head, I answered: *That's what my dad tells me.*
90 *It'll have to do for you. Good morning, Louis.* I reached over and flipped the standby switch, which kept the computer ready but not actively running. **D**

I showered, dressed, and picked up the printout of my history project. As I was about to leave the room, I glanced back at the computer table. Had I been imagining things?

I'll have to ask Dad about it when he calls tonight, I thought. *I wonder what he'll think of it. Bad enough the thing is talking to me. I'm answering it!*

Before I went out to catch my bus, I carefully checked the
100 house for unlocked doors and open windows. It was part of my daily routine. Mom works, and most of the day the house is empty: a natural setup for robbers. I glanced in the hall mirror just as I was ready to go out the door.

My usual reflection gazed back. Same old Kevin Neal: five ten, one hundred twenty pounds, light-brown hair, gray eyes, clear skin. I was wearing my Santa Rosario Rangers T-shirt, jeans, and sneakers.

"You don't look like a flake to me," I said to the mirror, then added, "but maybe Mom's right. Maybe you spend too much time
110 alone with Louis." Then I ran to get my bus. **E**

Ginny Linke was just two seats away from me on the bus. She was with Sherry Graber and Linda Martinez. They were laughing, whispering to each other, and looking around at the other students. I promised myself that today I was actually going to talk to Ginny. But then, I'd promised myself that every day for the past school year. Somehow I'd never got up the nerve.

What does she want to talk with you for? I asked myself. *She's great-looking . . . has that head of blond hair . . . a terrific bod, and wears the latest clothes. . . .*

D LANGUAGE COACH

The word *actively* is an **adverb** that describes the verb *running*. Continue reading and see if you can find another adverb on this page. Remember that adverbs only describe verbs. Write the adverb you find and its meaning.

_____

_____

_____

_____

E READ AND DISCUSS

Comprehension
How does Kevin's mother's comment fit in with what you know about Kevin?

And just look at yourself, pal, I thought. You're under six foot, skinny . . . a year younger than most kids in junior high. Worse than that, you're a brain. If that doesn't ace you out with girls, what does? Ⓐ

Ⓐ **LITERARY FOCUS**

Briefly describe Kevin's feelings for Ginny and about himself. What possible **theme** of this story do they suggest?

_____

_____

_____

_____

_____

_____

_____

_____

_____

_____

The bus stopped in front of Santa Rosario High and the students began to file out. I got up fast and quickly covered the space between me and Ginny Linke. *It's now or never*, I thought. I reached forward and tapped Ginny on the shoulder. She turned and smiled. She really smiled!

"Uhhhh . . . Ginny?" I said.

130 "Yes, what is it?" she replied.

"I'm Kevin Neal. . . ."

"Yes, I know," said Ginny.

"You do?" I gulped in amazement. "How come?"

"I asked my brother, Chuck. He's in your math class."

I knew who Chuck Linke was. He plays left tackle on the Rangers. The only reason he's in my math class is he's taken intermediate algebra twice . . . so far. He's real bad news, and I stay clear of him and his crowd.

"What'd you ask Chuck?" I said.

140 Ginny laughed. "I asked him who was that nerdy kid who keeps staring at me on the bus. He knew who I meant, right away."

Sherry and Linda, who'd heard it all, broke into squeals of laughter. They were still laughing and looking back over their shoulders at me when they got off the bus. I slunk off the vehicle, feeling even more nerdish than Ginny thought I was.

When I got home that afternoon, at two, I went right into the empty house. I avoided my reflection in the hall mirror. I was pretty sure I'd screwed up on the fourth-period math test. All I

150 could see was Ginny's face, laughing at me. Ⓑ

Nerdy kid, I thought, *that's what she thinks of me*. I didn't even have my usual after-school snack of a peanut butter and banana sandwich. I went straight upstairs to my room and tossed

Ⓑ **READING FOCUS**

Based on his actions, how does Kevin feel about himself now? How do those feelings **compare** to how he felt before he talked to Ginny?

_____

_____

_____

_____

my books onto the unmade bed. I walked over to the computer table and pushed the *on* button. The screen flashed:

Good afternoon, Kevin.

Although it wasn't the programmed response to Louis's greeting, I typed in: *There's nothing good about it. And girls are no @#%!!! good!* The machine responded:

160   Don't use bad language, Kevin. It isn't nice.

Repeat last message, I typed rapidly. It was happening again! The machine was . . . well, it was talking to me, like another person would. The "bad language" message disappeared and in its place was: **C**

Once is enough, Kevin. Don't swear at me for something I didn't do.

"This is it," I said aloud. "I'm losing my marbles." **D** I reached over to flip the standby switch. Louis's screen quickly flashed out:

170   Don't cut me off, Kevin. Maybe I can help: Y/N?

I punched the *Y*. "If I'm crazy," I said, "at least I have company. Louis doesn't think I'm a nerd. Or does it?" The machine flashed the message:

How can I help?

Do you think I'm a nerd? I typed.

Never! I think you're wonderful. Who said you were a nerd? **E**

I stared at the screen. *How do you know what a nerd is?* I typed. The machine responded instantly. It had never run this

180 fast before.

Special vocabulary, entry #635. BASIC Prog. #4231. And who said you were a nerd?

"That's right," I said, relieved. "Dad programmed all those extra words for Louis's 'personality.'" Then I typed in the answer to Louis's question: *Ginny Linke said it.* Louis flashed:

This is a human female? Request additional data.

Still not believing I was doing it, I entered all I knew about Ginny Linke, right down to the phone number I'd never had the

LANGUAGE COACH

Identify the **adverb** in this paragraph.

_____

_____

VOCABULARY

Word Study

The phrase "I'm losing my marbles," is an idiom that means, "I'm going crazy." An idiom is an expression whose meaning cannot be understood from the meanings of the individual words. Another example would be, "it's raining cats and dogs." Name another idiom. What does it mean?

_____

_____

_____

_____

_____

LITERARY FOCUS

How do Louis's feelings about Kevin differ from Ginny's feelings about Kevin? How does this help you understand the **theme** of the story?

_____

_____

_____

_____

190 nerve to use. Maybe it was dumb, but I also typed in how I felt about Ginny. I even wrote out the incident on the bus that morning. Louis whirred, then flashed out:

She's cruel and stupid. You're the finest person I know.

I'm the ONLY person you know, I typed.

That doesn't matter. You are my user. Your happiness is everything to me. I'll take care of Ginny.

The screen returned to the *Good afternoon, Kevin* message. I typed out: *Wait! How can you do all this? What do you mean, you'll take care of Ginny?* But all Louis responded was:

Programming Error: 76534. Not programmed to respond to
200 this type of question. **A**

No matter what I did for the next few hours, I couldn't get Louis to do anything outside of its regular programming. When Mom came home from work, I didn't mention the funny goings-on. I was sure Mom would think I'd gone stark bonkers. But

© James Porto/Getty Images

when Dad called that evening, after dinner, I asked to speak to him.

"Hi, Dad. How's Chicago?"

"Dirty, crowded, cold, and windy," came Dad's voice over the miles. "But did you want a weather report, son? What's on your mind? Something wrong?"

"Not exactly, Dad. Louis is acting funny. Real funny."

"Shouldn't be. I checked it out just before I left. Remember you were having trouble with the modem? You couldn't get Louis to access any of the mainframe databanks."

"That's right!" I said. "I forgot about that."

"Well, I didn't," Dad said. "I patched in our latest modem model. Brand-new. You can leave a question on file and when Louis can access the databanks at the cheapest time, it'll do it automatically. It'll switch from standby to on, get the data, then return to standby, after it saves what you asked. Does that answer your question?"

"Uhhhh . . . yeah, I guess so, Dad."

"All right, then. Let me talk to your mom now." **B**

I gave the phone to Mom and walked upstairs while she and Dad were still talking. The modem, I thought. Of course. That was it. The modem was a telephone link to any number of huge computers at various places all over the country. So Louis could get all the information it wanted at any time, so long as the standby switch was on. Louis was learning things at an incredible rate by picking the brains of the giant computers. **C** And Louis had a hard disk memory that could store 100 million bytes of information.

But that still didn't explain the unprogrammed responses . . . the "conversation" I'd had with the machine. **D** Promising myself I'd talk more about it with Dad, I went to bed. It had been a rotten day and I was glad to see the end of it come. I woke next morning in a panic. I'd forgotten to set my alarm. Dressing frantically and skipping breakfast, I barely made my bus.

As I got on board, I grabbed a front seat. They were always empty. All the kids that wanted to talk and hang out didn't sit up

B READ AND DISCUSS

Comprehension

What does the conversation reveal about Kevin's father?

C LANGUAGE COACH

Remember that **adverbs** describe verbs. Name an adverb that means the same as "at an incredible rate" that could describe how Louis was learning things.

D READ AND DISCUSS

Comprehension

What is the big deal with the modem? **Follow-up:** What does Kevin think of the "conversation" he had with Louis?

front where the driver could hear them. I saw Ginny, Linda, and Sherry in the back. Ginny was staring at me and she didn't look too happy. Her brother Chuck, who was seated near her, glared at me too. What was going on?

Once the bus stopped at the school, it didn't take long to find out. I was walking up the path to the main entrance when someone grabbed me from behind and spun me around. I found myself nose to nose with Chuck Linke. This was not a pleasant prospect. Chuck was nearly twice my size. Even the other guys on
250   the Rangers refer to him as "The Missing" Linke. And he looked real ticked off.

"OK, nerd," growled Chuck, "what's the big idea?"

"Energy and mass are different aspects of the same thing?" I volunteered, with a weak smile. "E equals MC squared.[7] That's the biggest idea I know."

"Don't get wise, nerd," Chuck said. He grabbed my shirt front and pulled me to within inches of his face. I couldn't help but notice that Chuck needed a shave. And Chuck was only fifteen!
260   "Don't play dumb," Chuck went on. "I mean those creepy phone calls. Anytime my sister gets on the phone, some voice cuts in and says things to her."

"What kind of things?" I asked, trying to get loose.

"You know very well what they are. Ginny told me about talking to you yesterday. You got some girl to make those calls for you and say all those things. . . . So you and your creepy girlfriend better knock it off. Or I'll knock _you_ off. Get it?" A

For emphasis Chuck balled his free hand into a fist the size of a ham and held it under my nose. I didn't know what he was
270   talking about, but I had to get away from this moose before he did me some real harm.

---

7. **E equals MC squared:** reference to Albert Einstein's famous equation describing the relationship between energy and mass. This equation transformed the field of physics.

"First off, I don't have a girlfriend, creepy or otherwise," I said. "And second, I don't know what you're talking about. And third, you better let me go, Chuck Linke."

"Oh, yeah? Why should I?"

"Because if you look over your shoulder, you'll see the assistant principal is watching us from his office window."

Chuck released me and spun around. There was no one at the window. But by then I was running to the safety of the school
280 building. I figured the trick would work on him. For Chuck the hard questions begin with "How are you?" I hid out from him for the rest of the day and walked home rather than chance seeing the monster on the bus. **B**

Louis's screen was dark when I ran upstairs to my bedroom. I placed a hand on the console. It was still warm. I punched the *on* button, and the familiar *Good afternoon, Kevin* was displayed.

Don't good afternoon me, I typed furiously. **C** *What have you done to Ginny Linke?* Louis's screen replied:

Programming Error: 76534. Not programmed to respond to
290 this type of question.

Don't get cute, I entered. *What are you doing to Ginny? Her brother nearly knocked my head off today.* Louis's screen responded immediately.

Are you hurt: Y/N?

No, I'm okay. But I don't know for how long. I've been hiding out from Chuck Linke today. He might catch me tomorrow, though. Then, I'll be history! The response from Louis came instantly.

Your life is in danger: Y/N?

I explained to Louis that my life wasn't really threatened.
300 But it sure could be made very unpleasant by Chuck Linke. Louis flashed:

This Chuck Linke lives at same address as the Ginny Linke person: Y/N?

I punched in *Y*. Louis answered.

Don't worry then. HE'S history!

B READ AND DISCUSS

Comprehension
What is going on with the Linke family?

C VOCABULARY

Selection Vocabulary
Furiously is an adverb that is based on the word *furious*. Look up the different meanings of the word *furious*. How might more than one of these definitions make sense in describing Kevin in this scene?

_____

_____

_____

_____

_____

_____

A **READ AND DISCUSS**

Comprehension

When and why does Louis stop responding as Louis and start behaving like a regular computer?

B **LITERARY FOCUS**

How does what is happening here connect to the **theme**?

Wait! What are you going to do? I wrote. But Louis only answered with: _Programming Error: 76534._ And nothing I could do would make the machine respond. . . . **A**

"Just what do you think you're doing, Kevin Neal?"
310 demanded Ginny Linke. She had cornered me as I walked up the path to the school entrance. Ginny was really furious.

"I don't know what you're talking about," I said, a sinking feeling settling in my stomach. I had an idea that I _did_ know. I just wasn't sure of the particulars.

"Chuck was arrested last night," Ginny said. "Some Secret Service men came to our house with a warrant. They said he'd sent a telegram threatening the president's life. They traced it right to our phone. He's still locked up. . . ." Ginny looked like she was about to cry.

320 "Then this morning," she continued, "we got two whole truckloads of junk mail! Flyers from every strange company in the world. Mom got a notice that all our credit cards have been canceled. And the Internal Revenue Service has called Dad in for an audit! I don't know what's going on, Kevin Neal, but somehow I think you've got something to do with it!"

"But I didn't . . ." I began, but Ginny was striding up the walk to the main entrance.

I finished the school day, but it was a blur. Louis had done it, all right. It had access to mainframe computers. It also had the
330 ability to try every secret access code to federal and commercial memory banks until it got the right one. Louis had cracked their security systems. It was systematically destroying the entire Linke family, and all via telephone lines! What would it do next? **B**

More important, I thought, what would _I_ do next? It's one thing to play a trick or two, to get even, but Louis was going crazy! And I never wanted to harm Ginny, or even her stupid moose of a brother. She'd just hurt my feelings with that nerd remark.

"You have to disconnect Louis," I told myself. "There's no
340 other way."

But why did I feel like such a rat about doing it? I guess because Louis was my friend . . . the only one I had. "Don't be a jerk," I went on. "Louis is a machine. He's a very wonderful, powerful machine. And it seems he's also very dangerous. You have to pull its plug, Kevin!" **C**

I suddenly realized that I'd said the last few words aloud. Kids around me on the bus were staring. I sat there feeling like the nerd Ginny thought I was, until my stop came. I dashed from the bus and ran the three blocks to my house.

350   When I burst into the hall, I was surprised to see my father, coming from the kitchen with a cup of coffee in his hand.

"Dad! What are you doing here?"

"Some kids say hello," Dad replied. "Or even, 'Gee, it's good to see you, Dad.'"

"I'm sorry, Dad," I said. "I didn't expect anyone to be home at this hour."

"Wound up my business in Chicago a day sooner than I expected," he said. "But what are you all out of breath about? Late for something?"

360   "No, Dad," I said. "It's Louis. . . ."

"Not to worry. I had some time on my hands, so I checked it out again. You were right. It was acting very funny. I think it had to do with the in-built logic/growth program I designed for it. You know . . . the 'personality' thing? Took me a couple of hours to clean the whole system out."

"To what?" I cried. **D**

"I erased the whole program and set Louis up as a normal computer. Had to disconnect the whole thing and do some rewiring. It had been learning, all right. But it was also turning

370   itself around. . . ." Dad stopped, and looked at me. "It's kind of involved, Kevin," he said. "Even for a bright kid like you. Anyway, I think you'll find Louis is working just fine now.

"Except it won't answer you as Louis anymore. It'll only function as a regular Major Electronics Model Z-11127. I guess the personality program didn't work out."

C READ AND DISCUSS

Comprehension

What does Kevin think of Louis's actions? **Follow-up:** If Kevin realizes that he must stop Louis, why does he say he feels "like such a rat about doing it"?

D READING FOCUS

Compare what Kevin thinks about Louis with what Kevin's father thinks about Louis.

_____

_____

_____

_____

A **READ AND DISCUSS**

Comprehension

Kevin said there were tears in his eyes and he couldn't explain them to his father or himself. What does he mean by that?

B **READING FOCUS**

Briefly summarize the story, and explain its main topic and **theme**.

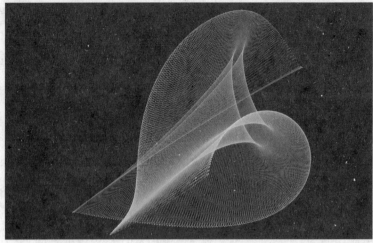

© Akira Inoue/amana images/Getty Images

I felt like a great weight had been taken off my shoulders. I didn't have to "face" Louis, and pull its plug. But somehow, all I could say was "Thanks, Dad."

"Don't mention it, son," Dad said brightly. He took his cup 380 of coffee and sat down in his favorite chair in the living room. I followed him.

"One more thing that puzzles me, though," Dad said. He reached over to the table near his chair. He held up three sheets of fanfold computer paper covered with figures. "Just as I was doing the final erasing, I must have put the printer on by accident. There was some data in the print buffer memory and it printed out. I don't know what to make of it. Do you?"

I took the papers from my father and read: *How do I love thee? Let me compute the ways:*[8] The next two pages were 390 covered with strings of binary code figures. On the last page, in beautiful color graphics,[9] was a stylized heart. Below it was the simple message: *I will always love you, Kevin: Louise.*

"Funny thing," Dad said. "It spelled its own name wrong."

"Yeah," I said. I turned and headed for my room. There were tears in my eyes and I knew I couldn't explain them to Dad, or myself either. A B

---

8. **How do I . . . ways:** reference to a famous poem by the English poet Elizabeth Barrett Browning (1806–1861) that begins, "How do I love thee? Let me count the ways."
9. **graphics:** designs or pictures.

User Friendly

USE A CHAIN OF EVENTS CHART

DIRECTIONS: Events that occur late in a story have more meaning because of their relation to events that occured earlier in the story. The sequence, or chain of events in a story is, therefore, very important. Use the following graphic organizer as a model for listing the main events that take place in "User Friendly" in the order that they happened.

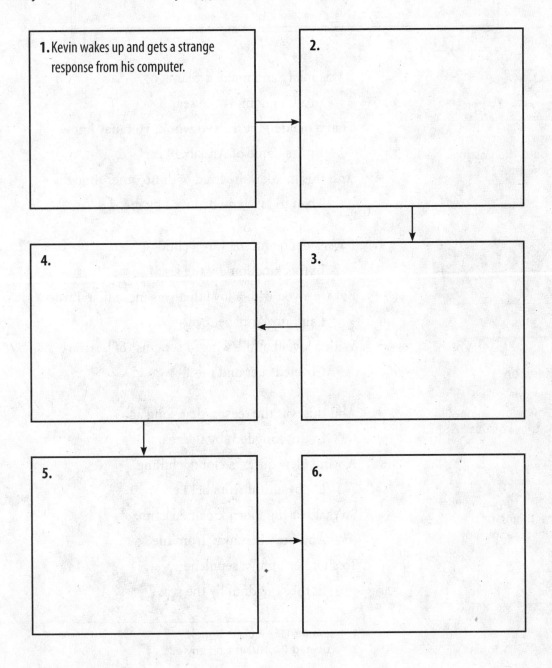

1. Kevin wakes up and gets a strange response from his computer.

2.

3.

4.

5.

6.

ANNABEL LEE

by Edgar Allan Poe

BACKGROUND

Seeking relief from loneliness and despair, Poe married his cousin, Virginia Clemm, when she was thirteen and he was twenty-six. Twelve years after they were married, Virginia died of tuberculosis, then known as "consumption." Poe wrote this poem after her death.

A LITERARY FOCUS

What does the first verse tell you about the possible **theme** of the poem?

_____

_____

_____

_____

B READ AND DISCUSS

Comprehension

What is the author setting up for you? **Follow-up:** What did the angels think of this love?

C LITERARY FOCUS

How does this turn of events change the **theme** of the poem? Is it still about love?

_____

_____

It was many and many a year ago,
        In a kingdom by the sea,
That a maiden there lived whom you may know
        By the name of Annabel Lee;
5   And this maiden she lived with no other thought
        Than to love and be loved by me. **A**

I was a child and *she* was a child,
        In this kingdom by the sea:
But we loved with a love that was more than love—
10   I and my Annabel Lee—
With a love that the wingèd seraphs[1] of heaven
        Coveted[2] her and me. **B**

And this was the reason that, long ago,
        In this kingdom by the sea,
15   A wind blew out of a cloud, chilling
        My beautiful Annabel Lee;
So that her highborn kinsmen came
        And bore her away from me,
To shut her up in a sepulcher
20   In this kingdom by the sea. **C**

---

1. **seraphs** (SEHR UHFS): angels.
2. **coveted** (KUHV IHT IHD): envied.

The angels, not half so happy in heaven,
    Went envying her and me—
Yes!—that was the reason (as all men know,
    In this kingdom by the sea)
25 That the wind came out of the cloud by night,
    Chilling and killing my Annabel Lee. **D**

But our love it was stronger by far than the love
    Of those who were older than we—
    Of many far wiser than we—
30 And neither the angels in heaven above,
    Nor the demons down under the sea,
Can ever dissever[3] my soul from the soul
    Of the beautiful Annabel Lee— **E**

For the moon never beams, without bringing me dreams
35   Of the beautiful Annabel Lee;
And the stars never rise, but I feel the bright eyes
    Of the beautiful Annabel Lee;
And so, all the night-tide, I lie down by the side
Of my darling—my darling—my life and my bride,
40   In the sepulcher there by the sea,
    In her tomb by the sounding sea. **F** **G**

---

3. **dissever** (DIH SEHV UHR): separate.

D (READ AND DISCUSS)

Comprehension

How does this new information connect with what we already know about the angels?

E (READ AND DISCUSS)

Comprehension

What does the speaker mean when he says nothing could "dissever" his soul from the soul of Annabel Lee?

F (VOCABULARY)

Word Study

Circle the word in this verse that is a synonym of the word *sepulcher*.

G (LITERARY FOCUS)

Briefly summarize this poem, and explain its topic and **theme**.

_____
_____
_____
_____
_____
_____
_____
_____
_____
_____

Skills Practice

User Friendly *and* Annabel Lee

USE A VENN DIAGRAM

DIRECTIONS: "User Friendly" and "Annabel Lee" share the **theme** of love. Each author, however, has different things to say about love. Use the chart below to help you understand the similarities and differences between the ways each author addresses the theme of love. Write the differences in the outer areas of the circles and write the similarities in the area where the circles overlap.

User Friendly   **Annabel Lee**

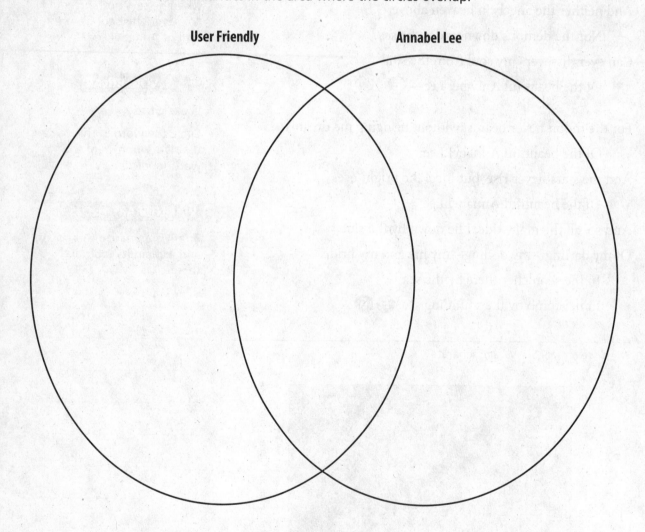

Applying Your Skills

User Friendly *and* Annabel Lee

VOCABULARY DEVELOPMENT

DIRECTIONS: Choose the two synonyms (words with similar meanings) that match each vocabulary word. Write the letters on the blank lines.

_____ **1.** absently
_____ **2.** furiously

a. absentmindedly
b. quickly
c. inattentively
d. intensely

LITERARY FOCUS: RECURRING THEMES ACROSS GENRES

DIRECTIONS: Describe the recurring **theme** in "User Friendly" and "Annabel Lee." Then give examples from each selection that support your choice.

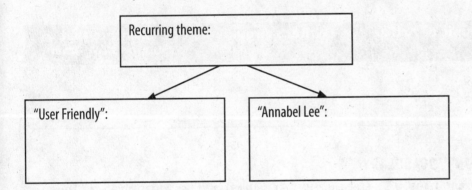

Recurring theme:

"User Friendly":

"Annabel Lee":

READING FOCUS: COMPARING THEMES

DIRECTIONS: Study the story chart you made for "Annabel Lee" and "User Friendly." Use the information you recorded to answer the questions.

1. How are the themes of each story similar?

_____

_____

2. How are the themes of each story different?

_____

_____

Literary Skills
Identify recurring themes in different genres.

Reading Skills
Compare and contrast themes.

Virtual Sticks and Stones

by The World Almanac

INFORMATIONAL TEXT FOCUS: PRESENTING AN ARGUMENT

Writers who present an **argument**, a debate or discussion, often want to convince you to accept or reject the argument, or act in a certain way. They may want you to buy their products, support a cause, or vote for a certain candidate.

Writers may use **anecdotes**, or brief stories, to make a point. In general, you should only accept arguments that have strong **evidence**. Evidence includes **facts** (statements that can be proved true), **statistics** (number facts), and quotes from **experts** on a subject.

As you read "Virtual Sticks and Stones" fill in a table like the one below with notes on the topic of the article, the argument being made by the writer, and the evidence used to support that argument.

Topic of Article	Writer's Argument	Evidence that Supports Argument

SELECTION VOCABULARY

misrepresentations (MIHS REHP RIH ZEHN TAY SHUHNZ) *n.*: false ideas given for the purpose of deceiving someone.
Some bullies make misrepresentations about their targets.

consequences (KAHN SUH KWENS IHZ) *n.*: results caused by a set of conditions.
Bullies are often afraid to face the consequences of their actions.

WORD STUDY

DIRECTIONS: Fill in the blanks with the correct vocabulary words to complete the paragraph.

People who make up online personalities may create

(1) _____ in an effort to make themselves more popular.

However they often ignore the (2) _____ that their actions

may have.

VIRTUAL STICKS AND STONES

by The World Almanac

> **BACKGROUND**
> "Virtual Sticks and Stones" is a newspaper article about bullying on the Internet, also called *cyberbullying.* As more young people use the Internet, cyberbullying has become a greater concern. In addition to evidence, the writer uses anecdotes from several young people to help make a point about the effects of bullying.

Chicago, Ill., Oct. 11 My first time typing words on a computer screen, I goofed and had to find the Delete key. Still, those first clicks and blips felt pretty powerful. Onscreen, my thoughts seemed to organize themselves. It became easier to write things quickly. Did you feel that way? Once you start communicating over the Internet, the world opens even wider. Suddenly, you don't have to see friends or call people to talk. It's all very exciting.

Maybe you, too, were like Katie in the beginning: "I was thrilled with the idea that I now had access to all aspects of the
10 Internet," writes Katie, 14, for Teen Angels, a youth group that works to combat Internet abuse. "The promising new window the Internet opened up for me seemed too good to be true, and in fact, it was." **A**

Online Threats

Katie was 9 when she first started to message people. She was home alone when she received an unforgettable note from a stranger. The words "Hold on; I'm coming after you" popped up from a screen name she did not know. Why would she read a message from someone with a screen name she did not know? She was new to the Internet and didn't know better. She
20 does now.

A (READING FOCUS)

Based only on the first two paragraphs, what do you think the writer's **argument** is?

_____

_____

_____

_____

_____

_____

A **READ AND DISCUSS**

Comprehension
What has the author set up for you? **Follow-up:** How has Katie handled her experience?

B **READING FOCUS**

What **statistics** do you see in this paragraph? How do they support the writer's **argument?**

_____

_____

_____

_____

_____

_____

C **READING FOCUS**

What form of **evidence** is the writer using here to support the **argument** being made about cyberbullying?

_____

_____

_____

© Ryan McVay/Getty Images

The threat scared Katie, and she hid in her room until her mom came home. She kept the incident to herself for a while, afraid that her parents would take away her Internet privileges. Now she talks about it as a way to get other kids to talk about cyberbullies. **A**

Cyberbullying Statistics

A threat like this is extreme, but we all know of someone who was burned on the Internet. In May 2006, two professors of criminal justice, one at Florida Atlantic University and one at the University of Wisconsin—Eau Claire, released results of a study
30 of 1,388 youths. One-third of those surveyed said they had been victims of cyberbullying. Another survey, from i-Safe America, says 60 percent of middle-school kids have been sent hurtful messages. **B**

"Little-noticed cyberbullying is the fastest-growing trend in bullying among teens," wrote Iris Salters, the Michigan Education Association president, in a recent editorial. **C**

Hidden Personalities

Some Web sites encourage people to create a Web personality, which can be very different from a person's real personality. Once invisible behind a new personality, cyberbullies can write
40 misrepresentations on buddy profiles, spill personal secrets about former friends, and join combative cliques that can attack under an assumed name. Because those who bully online are physically distant from their targets, they can feel more confident.

One seventh-grader I know was in a band that had a page on a social networking site. A kid hacked in and wrote violent threats that sounded as if band members had written them on the page. This hacker hid behind his victims' personalities. When Web personalities act in ways that real ones never would, they become a way to hide from truth, from consequences, and mostly from themselves. **D** **E**

50

Interpreting Web Behavior

Because cyberbullying appears in words, many people discount the damage it does. Sure, a good portion of online comments are meant in jest, so many people think, "What's the big deal?" Cyberbullying, however, doesn't come across as harmless to the target or to those who read the attack. Comments online may be written to be funny or to be cruel. It's hard to sense attempts at humor in a computer message. If someone passes by you in the school hallway and calls you a name, you can turn to him or her. Maybe the kid smiles to show it was meant in fun.

60 Maybe not. Being face to face reflects reality, keeping intent in perspective. **F**

Online Responsibility

The First Amendment to the U.S. Constitution guarantees freedom of speech, but there are laws to protect people from verbal and written abuse. Many schools already have in place policies regarding cyberabuse and punishments for students who attack others through e-mails, Web posts, and text messages.

If you are being bullied online, don't just take it. Tell an adult—a teacher, a parent, or a coach. Don't let a friend be cyberbullied. Urge them to get help.

70 Handle yourself responsibly online: Think about the people on the receiving end of your messages. Would you like the virtual sticks and stones of lies about you or your friends or family circulating throughout the Internet? **G**

D **VOCABULARY**

Selection Vocabulary

Think about the definition of *consequences.* Why would some people want to hide from the consequences of what they write on the Web?

_____

_____

_____

E **READING FOCUS**

This paragraph is an example of an **anecdote.** Do you think it helps make an argument about the negative effects of cyberbullying? Why or why not?

_____

_____

_____

F **READ AND DISCUSS**

Comprehension

What does the author mean by "being face to face reflects reality, keeping intent in perspective"?

G **READING FOCUS**

How does this question help the writer make an **argument** against cyberbullying?

_____

_____

_____

Virtual Sticks and Stones

USE A CHART

DIRECTIONS: Recall that when writers present an **argument**, they can use **anecdotes** or evidence such as **facts**, **statistics**, and **quotes** from experts. Use the chart below to identify specific examples of each type from the article.

How argument is presented	Example in article
facts	
statistics	
quotes from experts	
anecdotes	

Applying Your Skills

Virtual Sticks and Stones

VOCABULARY DEVELOPMENT

DIRECTIONS: Fill in the blanks with vocabulary words from the Word Box. You will use some terms more than once.

Word Box

misrepresentations
consequences

1. To be fair to other people, you should avoid writing _____ of things they have said or done.

2. Not studying can have serious _____ when you have to take a test.

3. If you lie about others, you need to be prepared to face the _____ of what you have done.

4. Some people do not realize that _____ of other people can hurt feelings.

INFORMATIONAL TEXT FOCUS: PRESENTING AN ARGUMENT

DIRECTIONS: Write one sentence stating the **argument** the writer presents in the article. Then, list three pieces of **evidence** that support this argument.

Argument:

_____

_____

Evidence:

1. _____

_____

_____

2. _____

_____

_____

3. _____

_____

_____

SKILLS FOCUS

Reading Skills
Understand how arguments are presented.

Collection 4

VOCABULARY REVIEW

DIRECTIONS: Choose the vocabulary word from the Word Box that best completes each sentence. Write the word on the blank line. Some of the words will not be used.

Word Box

absently

consequences

dismally

egotism

fundamental

furiously

habitual

implicit

intricate

misrepresentations

relevant

reveal

simultaneously

1. Kevin did not want to _____ the truth about Louis to his father.

2. He stared _____ out the window, not noticing the cars going by.

3. To support an argument, you must use _____ facts that relate to the argument.

4. Bragging about yourself is an example of _____ and may annoy others.

5. Louis's complex plans for revenge were quite _____ in nature.

6. Kevin had a _____ morning routine that he followed each day.

7. At first, Louise did not tell Kevin she loved him, but her feelings were _____ in her actions.

8. The _____ of the angels' actions were terrible for Annabel Lee.

9. When Jimmy and Bob looked at each other _____ under the light, Bob could tell that it wasn't really Jimmy at all.

10. Writing _____ about others can hurt their feelings.

Skills Review

Collection 4

DIRECTIONS: Four of the words listed in the Word Box are **adverbs**—*absently, dismally, furiously,* and *simultaneously.* Adverbs are words that modify, or change, verbs. The adverb in the sentence below is boldfaced. On the blank line, tell how the adverb changes the sentence.

Tom **angrily** hung up the phone. _____

_____

DIRECTIONS: Many adverbs end in *–ly.* Try adding the *–ly* ending to the other vocabulary words in the Word Box on the previous page. Which words become real adverbs and what do they mean? Write your answers below and check them in a dictionary.

_____

_____

_____

_____

_____

WRITING ACTIVITY

When you are presenting or trying to understand an argument, it is important to tell the difference between **facts** (statements that can be proven true) and opinions (a personal view that cannot be proven true). For example, if you describe Kevin Neal as a young man who has a computer, you are reporting a *fact.* If you say he should not have let Ginny hurt his feelings, you are offering your *opinion.*

DIRECTIONS: Choose one of the following selections: "After Twenty Years," "Annabel Lee," "User Friendly," or "Virtual Sticks and Stones." Write a paragraph about your chosen selection that describes one fact about the reading and one opinion about it. In your paragraph, explain why one statement is a fact and the other statement is an opinion.

Elements of Nonfiction

Literary and Academic Vocabulary for Collection 5

---

ambiguous (AM BIHG YOO UHS) *adj.*: having more than one possible meaning; unclear.

The directions he wrote on how to get to his house were very ambiguous.

evident (EHV UH DUHNT) *adj.*: easy to see or understand; clear.

The first-person point of view is always evident from the use of the word I.

convey (KUHN VAY) *v.*: make known, communicate, express.

Authors can convey their views on a subject in many ways.

principal (PRIHN SUH PUHL) *adj.*: most important.

What is the principal lesson we can learn from this chapter?

biography (BY AH GRAH FEE) *n.*: the story of a real person's life, written by another person.

The professor wrote a biography of Abraham Lincoln.

essay (EH SAY) *n.*: a short piece of nonfiction that looks at a single subject or limited topic.

I wrote an essay about the American Revolution for class.

Preparing to Read

Names/Nombres

by Julia Alvarez

LITERARY FOCUS: SUBJECTIVE AND OBJECTIVE POINTS OF VIEW

Nonfiction writing can be described as subjective or objective. Writings with a **subjective point of view** express the personal feelings, thoughts, opinions, and judgments of the writer. Writing from the **objective point of view**, on the other hand, sticks to the facts. It presents information in an unbiased manner. Writers may combine subjective and objective details within the same text. It's your job to figure out which statements are subjective and which are objective.

Use the Skill   Read these passages, and identify them as examples of either subjective or objective writing. Place a check mark in the appropriate box.

Passage	Point of View	
McPhee Tower, built in 1949, burned to the ground Thursday morning. Investigators say the fire was caused by an electrical short in the building's wiring.	Subjective Objective	☐ ☐
Although some would disagree with me, I have to say that science writing is the most rewarding career a person could choose. No other job can compare.	Subjective Objective	☐ ☐

READING FOCUS: FINDING THE MAIN IDEA

The **main idea** is the central idea that a writer wants you to remember. All the important ideas in a text should add up to the main idea. Sometimes the main idea is implied, or suggested, by details rather than clearly stated. In such cases, you must **infer**, or guess, the main idea that the writer wants you to understand.

Use these tips to help you infer the main idea:

• Identify the important details.

• Think about the point that the details make.

• State the main idea in your own words.

SKILLS FOCUS

Literary Skills
Examine objective and subjective points of view.

Reading Skills
Find the main idea.

Vocabulary Development

Names/Nombres

SELECTION VOCABULARY

ethnicity (EHTH NIHS UH TEE) *n.:* common culture or nationality.

Julia's ethnicity was important to her friends.

exotic (EHG ZAHT IHK) *adj.:* not native.

At her graduation party, Julia's family served exotic dishes.

heritage (HEHR UH TIHJ) *n.:* traditions that are passed along.

Julia remained proud of her Dominican heritage.

convoluted (KAHN VUH LOO TIHD) *v.* used as *adj.:* complicated.

The grammar of a new language often seems convoluted.

WORD STUDY

Write "Yes" after each sentence if the boldfaced vocabulary word is used correctly. Write "No" if the word is used incorrectly, and rewrite the sentence so that it is used correctly.

1. My father was proud of his **ethnicity**, so he maintained many traditions of his homeland after moving to the United States. _____

   _____

   _____

2. Apple pie is an **exotic** dish in the United States. _____

   _____

   _____

3. My grandfather taught us to appreciate our family **heritage**. _____

   _____

   _____

4. The elementary math problems were **convoluted** for the high school students. _____

   _____

   _____

NAMES/NOMBRES

by Julia Alvarez

© Alexandra Heyes

A (READ AND DISCUSS)

Comprehension
What is evident, or clear, about the "Elbures" family?

When we arrived in New York City, our names changed almost immediately. At Immigration, the officer asked my father, *Mister Elbures*, if he had anything to declare. My father shook his head no, and we were waved through. I was too afraid we wouldn't be let in if I corrected the man's pronunciation, but I said our name to myself, opening my mouth wide for the organ blast of the *a*, trilling my tongue for the drumroll of the *r*, *All-vah-rrr-es*! How could anyone get *Elbures* out of that orchestra of sound? **A**

At the hotel my mother was Missus Alburest, and I was *little*
10 *girl*, as in, "Hey, little girl, stop riding the elevator up and down. It's *not* a toy."

When we moved into our new apartment building, the super called my father *Mister Alberase*, and the neighbors who became mother's friends pronounced her name *Jew-lee-ah* instead of *Hoo-lee-ah*. I, her namesake, was known as *Hoo-lee-tah* at home. But at school I was *Judy* or *Judith*, and once an English teacher mistook me for *Juliet*.

It took a while to get used to my new names. I wondered if I shouldn't correct my teachers and new friends. But my
20 mother argued that it didn't matter. "You know what your friend Shakespeare said, '*A rose by any other name would smell as sweet*.'"[1] My family had gotten into the habit of calling any famous author "my friend" because I had begun to write poems and stories in English class.

By the time I was in high school, I was a popular kid, and it showed in my name. Friends called me *Jules* or *Hey Jude*, and once a group of troublemaking friends my mother forbade me to hang out with called me *Alcatraz*. **B** I was *Hoo-lee-tah* only to Mami and Papi and uncles and aunts who came over to
30 eat sancocho[2] on Sunday afternoons—old world folk whom I would just as soon go back to where they came from and leave me to pursue whatever mischief I wanted to in America. *JUDY ALCATRAZ*, the name on the "Wanted" poster would read. Who would ever trace her to me? **C** **D**

My older sister had the hardest time getting an American name for herself because *Mauricia* did not translate into English. Ironically, although she had the most foreign-sounding name, she and I were the Americans in the family. We had been born in New York City when our parents had first tried immigration and
40 then gone back "home," too homesick to stay. My mother often told the story of how she had almost changed my sister's name in the hospital.

After the delivery, Mami and some other new mothers were cooing over their new baby sons and daughters and

---

1. "*A rose . . . as sweet*": Julia's mother is quoting from the play *Romeo and Juliet*.
2. **sancocho** (SAHN KOH CHOH) *adj.:* stew of meats and fruit.

B VOCABULARY

Word Study

Alcatraz is an island off the coast of California. For decades, it was home to a federal prison. What does this information tell you about the friends who gave Julia this nickname?

_____

_____

_____

_____

C LITERARY FOCUS

Based on what you have read so far, would you classify this essay as an example of **subjective writing** or **objective** writing? Explain.

_____

_____

_____

_____

_____

D READ AND DISCUSS

Comprehension

When the "old world folk" came to visit, Julia wished they would go back to where they came from. What does that tell you about her?

A (**READ AND DISCUSS**)

Comprehension

What does the story about Mauricia's name tell you about the mother?

B (**READING FOCUS**)

Much attention has been focused so far on how the characters' Spanish names changed when they moved to the United States. Do you think this could be related to the story's **main idea**? Explain your answer.

exchanging names and weights and delivery stories. My mother was embarrassed among the Sallys and Janes and Georges and Johns to reveal the rich, noisy name of *Mauricia*, so when her turn came to brag, she gave her baby's name as *Maureen*.

"Why'd ya give her an Irish name with so many pretty Spanish names to choose from?" one of the women asked.

50 My mother blushed and admitted her baby's real name to the group. Her mother-in-law had recently died, she apologized, and her husband had insisted that the first daughter be named after his mother, *Mauran*. My mother thought it the ugliest name she had ever heard, and she talked my father into what she believed was an improvement, a combination of *Mauran* and her own mother's name, *Felicia*.

"Her name is *Mao-ree-shee-ah*," my mother said to the group of women.

"Why, that's a beautiful name," the new mothers cried. "*Moor-ee-sha, Moor-ee-sha*," they cooed into the pink blanket.
60 *Moor-ee-sha* it was when we returned to the States eleven years later. Sometimes, American tongues found even that mispronunciation tough to say and called her *Maria* or *Marsha* or *Maudy* from her nickname *Maury*. I pitied her. What an awful name to have to transport across borders! **A**

My little sister, Ana, had the easiest time of all. She was plain *Anne*—that is, only her name was plain, for she turned out to be the pale, blond "American beauty" in the family. The only Hispanic thing about her was the affectionate nicknames her boyfriends sometimes gave her. *Anita*, or, as one goofy guy
70 used to sing to her to the tune of the banana advertisement, *Anita Banana*.

Later, during her college years in the late sixties, there was a push to pronounce Third World[3] names correctly. I remember calling her long distance at her group house and a roommate answering. **B**

---

3. **Third World**: developing countries of Latin America, Africa, and Asia.

"Can I speak to Ana?" I asked, pronouncing her name the American way.

"Ana?" The man's voice hesitated. "Oh! You must mean *Ah-nah*!"

80 Our first few years in the States, though, ethnicity was not yet "in." **C** Those were the blond, blue-eyed, bobby-sock years of junior high and high school before the sixties ushered in peasant blouses, hoop earrings, serapes.[4] My initial desire to be known by my correct Dominican name faded. I just wanted to be Judy and merge with the Sallys and Janes in my class. **D** But, inevitably, my accent and coloring gave me away. "So where are you from, Judy?"

"New York," I told my classmates. After all, I had been born blocks away at Columbia-Presbyterian Hospital.

90 "I mean, *originally*."

"From the Caribbean," I answered vaguely, for if I specified, no one was quite sure on what continent our island was located.

"Really? I've been to Bermuda. We went last April for spring vacation. I got the worst sunburn! So, are you from Portoriko?"

"No," I sighed. "From the Dominican Republic."

"Where's that?"

"South of Bermuda."

They were just being curious, I knew, but I burned with shame whenever they singled me out as a "foreigner," a rare,
100 exotic friend. **E**

"Say your name in Spanish, oh, please say it!" I had made mouths drop one day by rattling off my full name, which, according to Dominican custom, included my middle names, Mother's and Father's surnames for four generations back.

"Julia Altagracia María Teresa Álvarez Tavares Perello Espaillat Julia Pérez Rochet González." I pronounced it slowly,

4. serapes (SAY RAH PAYS) *n.:* woolen shawls worn in some Latin American countries.

C LANGUAGE COACH

A **suffix** is a word part added to the end of a word. *Ethnicity* has the suffix *–ity*, which means "having a particular quality." What particular quality does *ethnicity* describe? Use a dictionary to check your answer.

_____

_____

_____

D READING FOCUS

What can you **infer** about Julia from her desire to be "Judy"?

_____

_____

_____

_____

_____

E VOCABULARY

Selection Vocabulary

Underline context clues that may hint at what *exotic* means, and then write the definition in your own words.

_____

_____

_____

_____

A **READ AND DISCUSS**

Comprehension
The author tells you that when she pronounces her name, she says it slowly. What point is she making?

B **VOCABULARY**

Selection Vocabulary
Considering what you've learned about the main character and her family so far, what do you think *heritage* means?

_____

_____

_____

C **VOCABULARY**

Academic Vocabulary
What do you think the author is trying to *convey*, or communicate, about friends and family in this story?

_____

_____

_____

a name as chaotic with sounds as a Middle Eastern bazaar or market day in a South American village. **A**

110 My Dominican heritage was never more apparent than when my extended family attended school occasions. **B** For my graduation, they all came, the whole lot of aunts and uncles and the many little cousins who snuck in without tickets. They sat in the first row in order to better understand the Americans' fast-spoken English. But how could they listen when they were constantly speaking among themselves in florid-sounding[5] phrases, rococo[6] consonants, rich, rhyming vowels?

Introducing them to my friends was a further trial to me. These relatives had such complicated names and there were so many of them, and their relationships to myself were so convo-

120 luted. There was my Tía[7] Josefina, who was not really an aunt but a much older cousin. And her daughter, Aida Margarita, who was adopted, una hija de crianza.[8] My uncle of affection, Tío José, brought my madrina[9] Tía Amelia and her comadre[10] Tía Pilar. My friends rarely had more than a "Mom and Dad" to introduce.

After the commencement ceremony, my family waited outside in the parking lot while my friends and I signed yearbooks with nicknames which recalled our high school good times: "Beans" and "Pepperoni" and "Alcatraz." We hugged and cried and promised to keep in touch.

130 Our goodbyes went on too long. I heard my father's voice calling out across the parking lot, "*Hoo-lee-tah*! Vámonos!"[11] **C**

---

5. **florid-sounding**: flowery; using fancy words.
6. **rococo** (RUH KOH KOH) *adj.:* fancy. Rococo is an early-eighteenth-century style of art and architecture known for its fancy ornamentation.
7. **Tía** (TEE AH) *n.:* Spanish for "aunt." *Tío* is "uncle."
8. **una hija de crianza** (OO NAH EE HAH DAY KREE AHN SAH): Spanish for "an adopted daughter." *Crianza* means "upbringing."
9. **madrina** (MAH DREE NAH) *n.:* Spanish for "godmother."
10. **comadre** (KOH MAH DRAY) *n.:* informal Spanish for "close friend." *Comadre* is the name used by the mother and the godmother of a child for each other.
11. **Vámonos!** (VAH MOH NOHS): Spanish for "Let's go!"

© Neville Elder/Corbis

Back home, my tíos and tías and primas,[12] Mami and Papi, and mis hermanas[13] had a party for me with sancocho and a store-bought pudín,[14] inscribed with *Happy Graduation, Julie.* There were many gifts—that was a plus to a large family! I got several wallets and a suitcase with my initials and a graduation charm from my godmother and money from my uncles. The biggest gift was a portable typewriter from my parents for writing my stories and poems.

140   Someday, the family predicted, my name would be well-known throughout the United States. I laughed to myself, wondering which one I would go by. D E

E READ AND DISCUSS

Comprehension
Julia laughs when she thinks about which "well-known" name she'll go by. What does this tell you about her?

---

12. **primas** (PREE MAHS) *n.:* Spanish for "female cousins."
13. **mis hermanas** (MEES EHR MAH NAHS): Spanish for "my sisters."
14. **pudín** (POO DEEN) *n.:* Spanish cake.

Skills Practice

Names/Nombres

USE A CHART

DIRECTIONS: Choose five different names from "Names/Nombres" that writer
Julia Alvarez was called by friends, family, acquaintances, or strangers. Then,
describe the special meaning that each name had. One name has been provided.

Name	Special meaning
1. Alcatraz	
2.	
3.	
4.	
5.	

Applying Your Skills

Names/Nombres

VOCABULARY DEVELOPMENT

DIRECTIONS: Fill in the correct vocabulary words from the Word Box to complete the paragraph. One word will not be used.

Word Box

ethnicity

exotic

heritage

convoluted

The Dominican Republic was foreign and (1) _____ to Julia's friends. Julia's family tree was so (2) _____ that even she had difficulty understanding it sometimes. Large celebrations were part of Julia's family (3) _____.

LITERARY FOCUS: SUBJECTIVE AND OBJECTIVE POINTS OF VIEW

DIRECTIONS: Examine the sentences below and decide if each shows an **objective** or **subjective point of view**. Write your answers on the blanks.

1. Julia's father had nothing to declare at Immigration. _____

2. One of Ana's boyfriends was a "goofy guy." _____

3. Julia's extended family attended school activities. _____

READING FOCUS: FINDING THE MAIN IDEA

DIRECTIONS: Complete the chart below by filling in the story's **main idea** and providing three details that support the main idea.

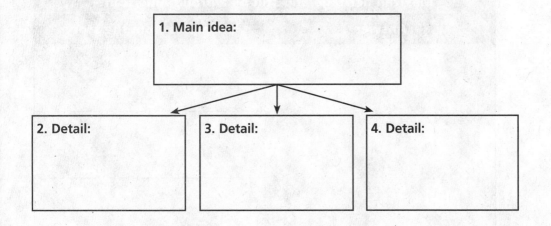

1. Main idea:

2. Detail:

3. Detail:

4. Detail:

Literary Skills
Distinguish between subjective and objective points of view.

Reading Skills
Make inferences to find the main idea.

from Barrio Boy

by Ernesto Galarza

LITERARY FOCUS: ANALYZING RESPONSES TO LITERATURE

A helpful way to understand a story's meaning is to **analyze** it by asking questions about the story as you read. Then, write down the answers you learn from the text. Your answers can be organized into a response to the story.

Write a Response   As you read this selection from *Barrio Boy*, one important question to ask yourself is, *How does Ernesto learn that "becoming a proud American" doesn't mean giving up his Mexican heritage?* After completing the Reading Focus exercise below, write a paragraph that answers this question. Later, you will share your answer with a classmate and analyze their response to the same question.

READING FOCUS: ORGANIZING INFORMATION

When you analyze a response to literature, you should consider how **focused** the answer is—how well it organizes information. An unsatisfying response will be based only on opinions or lack supporting details (pieces of information) from the text. A good response will include **textual support**, or details and examples from the text that support each main idea.

Use the Skill   As you read, use this chart to help organize the information you need in order to answer the following question about *Barrio Boy*:

Question: How does Ernesto discover that he can keep his Mexican heritage and still be a proud American?	
Answer	**Examples from the story**
	1.
	2.
	3.

Literary Skills
Analyze responses to literature.

Reading Skills
Organize information.

Vocabulary Development

from Barrio Boy

SELECTION VOCABULARY

reassuring (REE UH SHUR IHNG) *v.* used as *adj.*: comforting.
   Ernesto's teachers were kind and reassuring.

contraption (KUHN TRAP SHUHN) *n.*: strange machine or gadget.
   A contraption at the top of the door closed it automatically.

assured (UH SHURD) *v.*: guaranteed; promised confidently.
   Ernesto's teachers assured him that he would enjoy the new school.

formidable (FAWR MUH DUH BUHL) *adj.*: awe-inspiring, impressive.
   Miss Hopley's height made her seem formidable.

survey (SUHR VAY) *v.*: look carefully in order to make a decision or gather information.
   Ernesto sat down to survey his new class.

WORD STUDY

DIRECTIONS: The following words are antonyms of some of the selection vocabulary. Antonyms are words with opposite meanings. Write the correct vocabulary words next to their antonyms. One word will not be used.

   1. skim _____

   2. distressing _____

   3. unimpressive _____

   4. discouraged _____

from BARRIO BOY

by Ernesto Galarza

© Diana Ong/Superstock

From *Barrio Boy* by Ernesto Galarza. Copyright © 1971 by **University of Notre Dame Press.** Reproduced by permission of the publisher.

BACKGROUND

Ernesto Galarza came to the United States from Mexico as a young boy in the early 1900s. He had to learn a new language and new customs. Galarza found that education was the key to understanding his new world. He eventually became a professor and writer. The following selection is taken from his book *Barrio Boy*, written in 1971. *Barrio Boy* describes Ernesto's journey from Mexico to the United States.

A VOCABULARY

Selection Vocabulary

What clues does this sentence provide about the meaning of the word *contraption*?

_____

_____

_____

B READ AND DISCUSS

Comprehension

What has the author told you so far?

The two of us [Ernesto and his mother] walked south on Fifth Street one morning to the corner of Q Street and turned right. Half of the block was occupied by the Lincoln School. It was a three-story wooden building, with two wings that gave it the shape of a double T connected by a central hall. It was a new building, painted yellow, with a shingled roof that was not like the red tile of the school in Mazatlán. I noticed other differences, none of them very reassuring.

10   We walked up the wide staircase hand in hand and through the door, which closed by itself. A mechanical contraption screwed to the top shut it behind us quietly. **A**

Up to this point the adventure of enrolling me in the school had been carefully rehearsed. Mrs. Dodson had told us how to find it and we had circled it several times on our walks. Friends in the barrio explained that the director was called a principal, and that it was a lady and not a man. They assured us that there was always a person at the school who could speak Spanish. **B**

Exactly as we had been told, there was a sign on the door in both Spanish and English: "Principal." We crossed the hall and

20   entered the office of Miss Nettie Hopley.

Miss Hopley was at a roll-top desk to one side, sitting in a swivel chair that moved on wheels. There was a sofa against the opposite wall, flanked by two windows and a door that opened on a small balcony. Chairs were set around a table, and framed pictures hung on the walls of a man with long white hair and another with a sad face and a black beard.

The principal half turned in the swivel chair to look at us over the pinch glasses crossed on the ridge of her nose. **C** To do this, she had to duck her head slightly, as if she were about to step through a low doorway.

What Miss Hopley said to us we did not know, but we saw in her eyes a warm welcome, and when she took off her glasses and straightened up, she smiled wholeheartedly, like Mrs. Dodson. We were, of course, saying nothing, only catching the friendliness of her voice and the sparkle in her eyes while she said words we did not understand. She signaled us to the table. Almost tiptoeing across the office, I maneuvered myself to keep my mother between me and the gringo[1] lady. In a matter of seconds I had to decide whether she was a possible friend or a menace. **D** We sat down.

Then Miss Hopley did a formidable thing. She stood up. Had she been standing when we entered, she would have seemed tall. But rising from her chair, she soared. And what she carried up and up with her was a buxom superstructure, firm shoulders, a straight sharp nose, full cheeks slightly molded by a curved line along the nostrils, thin lips that moved like steel springs, and a high forehead topped by hair gathered in a bun. Miss Hopley was not a giant in body, but when she mobilized it to a standing position she seemed a match for giants. I decided I liked her.

She strode to a door in the far corner of the office, opened it, and called a name. A boy of about ten years appeared in the doorway. He sat down at one end of the table. He was brown like us, a plump kid with shiny black hair combed straight back, neat, cool, and faintly obnoxious.

---

1. **gringo** (GRIHNG GOH): someone who is northern American, non-Hispanic, or doesn't speak Spanish.

Word Study

The words *principal* and *principle* are homophones, which are words that sound alike but have different meanings and spellings. Look up the meaning of *principle* and use it in a sentence.

_____

_____

_____

D VOCABULARY

Word Study

You may be unfamiliar with the word *menace*. In this sentence, the word *friend* means the opposite of the word *menace*. What is the meaning of *menace*?

_____

_____

_____

© Polka Dot Images/Jupiter Images

Miss Hopley joined us with a large book and some papers in her hand. She, too, sat down and the questions and answers began by way of our interpreter. My name was Ernesto. My mother's name was Henriqueta. My birth certificate was in San Blas. Here was my last report card from the Escuela Municipal Numero 3 para Varones[2] of Mazatlán, and so forth. Miss Hopley put things down in the book and my mother signed a card. **A**

As long as the questions continued, Doña Henriqueta could stay and I was secure. Now that they were over, Miss Hopley saw her to the door, dismissed our interpreter, and without further ado took me by the hand and strode down the hall to Miss Ryan's first grade.

Miss Ryan took me to a seat at the front of the room, into which I shrank—the better to survey her. She was, to skinny, somewhat runty me, of a withering height when she patrolled the class. And when I least expected it, there she was, crouching by my desk, her blond, radiant face level with mine, her voice patiently maneuvering me over the awful idiocies of the English language. **B**

During the next few weeks Miss Ryan overcame my fears of tall, energetic teachers as she bent over my desk to help me with a word in the pre-primer. Step by step, she loosened me and my classmates from the safe anchorage of the desks for recitations at the blackboard and consultations at her desk. Frequently she burst into happy announcements to the whole class. "Ito can read a sentence," and small Japanese Ito, squint-eyed and shy, slowly read aloud while the class listened in wonder: "Come,

---

2. **Escuela Municipal Numero 3 para Varones:** Spanish for "Municipal School Number 3 for Boys."

Skipper, come. Come and run." The Korean, Portuguese, Italian, and Polish first-graders had similar moments of glory, no less shining than mine the day I conquered "butterfly," which I had been persistently pronouncing in standard Spanish as boo-ter-flee. "Children," Miss Ryan called for attention. "Ernesto has learned how to pronounce *butterfly*!" And I proved it with a perfect imitation of Miss Ryan. From that celebrated success, I was soon able to match Ito's progress as a sentence reader with "Come, butterfly, come fly with me." C

Like Ito and several other first-graders who did not know English, I received private lessons from Miss Ryan in the closet, a narrow hall off the classroom with a door at each end. Next to one of these doors Miss Ryan placed a large chair for herself and a small one for me. Keeping an eye on the class through the open door, she read with me about sheep in the meadow and a frightened chicken going to see the king, coaching me out of my phonetic ruts in words like *pasture, bow-wow-wow, hay,* and *pretty,* which to my Mexican ear and eye had so many unnecessary sounds and letters. She made me watch her lips and then close my eyes as she repeated words I found hard to read. When we came to know each other better, I tried interrupting to tell Miss Ryan how we said it in Spanish. It didn't work. She only said "oh" and went on with *pasture, bow-wow-wow,* and *pretty.* D It was as if in that closet we were both discovering together the secrets of the English language and grieving together over the tragedies of Bo-Peep. The main reason I was graduated with honors from the first grade was that I had fallen in love with Miss Ryan. Her radiant, no-nonsense character made us either afraid not to love her or love her so we would not be afraid, I am not sure which. It was not only that we sensed she was with it, but also that she was with us. E

Like the first grade, the rest of the Lincoln School was a sampling of the lower part of town, where many races made their home. My pals in the second grade were Kazushi, whose parents spoke only Japanese; Matti, a skinny Italian boy; and

C **LANGUAGE COACH**

Antonyms are words that mean the opposite of each other. Select three words from this paragraph and write them below, along with an antonym for each one.

_____

_____

_____

D **VOCABULARY**

Academic Vocabulary
What does this response *convey,* or show us, about Miss Ryan's teaching methods?

_____

_____

_____

E **READ AND DISCUSS**

Comprehension
How are things going for Ernesto?

READING FOCUS

How does this example provide **textual support** for the main idea of becoming an American?

_____

_____

_____

READ AND DISCUSS

Comprehension

The author says that the staff at Lincoln "warmed knowledge into us and roasted racial hatreds out of us." What does he mean by that?

LITERARY FOCUS

Now that you have read the selection, **analyze** the story to answer this question: How does Ernesto learn that becoming a proud American doesn't mean giving up his Mexican heritage?

_____

_____

_____

Manuel, a fat Portuguese who would never get into a fight but wrestled you to the ground and just sat on you. Our assortment of nationalities included Koreans, Yugoslavs, Poles, Irish, and home-grown Americans.

Miss Hopley and her teachers never let us forget why we were at Lincoln: for those who were alien, to become good Americans; for those who were so born, to accept the rest of us. Off the school grounds we traded the same insults we heard from our elders. On the playground we were sure to be marched up to the principal's office for calling someone a wop, a chink, a dago, or a greaser. **A** The school was not so much a melting pot as a griddle where Miss Hopley and her helpers warmed knowledge into us and roasted racial hatreds out of us. **B**

At Lincoln, making us into Americans did not mean scrubbing away what made us originally foreign. The teachers called us as our parents did, or as close as they could pronounce our names in Spanish or Japanese. No one was ever scolded or punished for speaking in his native tongue on the playground. Matti told the class about his mother's down quilt, which she had made in Italy with the fine feathers of a thousand geese. Encarnación acted out how boys learned to fish in the Philippines. I astounded the third grade with the story of my travels on a stagecoach, which nobody else in the class had seen except in the museum at Sutter's Fort. After a visit to the Crocker Art Gallery and its collection of heroic paintings of the golden age of California, someone showed a silk scroll with a Chinese painting. Miss Hopley herself had a way of expressing wonder over these matters before a class, her eyes wide open until they popped slightly. It was easy for me to feel that becoming a proud American, as she said we should, did not mean feeling ashamed of being a Mexican. **C**

Applying Your Skills

from Barrio Boy

VOCABULARY DEVELOPMENT

DIRECTIONS: Fill in the blanks with the correct vocabulary words from the Word Box.

Word Box

reassuring

contraption

assured

formidable

survey

1. No one had ever seen an invention like this _____ before.

2. The explorers climbed to the top of the hill to _____ the surrounding land.

3. The mountains were a _____ barrier that worried the pioneers.

4. The inspector _____ the family that the building was safe.

5. It is _____ to have a flashlight in the dark.

LITERARY FOCUS: ANALYZING RESPONSES TO LITERATURE

DIRECTIONS: Choose a partner and exchange your responses to the question, "How does Ernesto learn that becoming a proud American doesn't mean giving up his Mexican heritage?" Read your partner's response and write a short review of it. Did he or she provide examples of evidence and supporting details in his or her response? Write down what you liked best and least about their answer and why. Remember to be polite and courteous when you write your review.

READING FOCUS: ORGANIZING INFORMATION

DIRECTIONS: Study the chart you made for "*from* Barrio Boy" and review your answers to the Reading Focus questions in the selection. Use that information to help you answer the following questions on a separate sheet of paper:

1. What did Ernesto have in common with many other students at his school?

2. How did the teachers treat foreign students? How did those students treat each other?

3. At Lincoln School, what did it mean for the students to be made "into Americans"?

SKILLS FOCUS

Literary Skills
Analyze responses to literature.

Reading Skills
Organize information.

Canines to the Rescue

by Jonah Goldberg

INFORMATIONAL TEXT FOCUS: ANALYZING AN AUTHOR'S PERSPECTIVE

Perspective is a view on a subject. As you read a nonfiction text, it's important to understand the **author's perspective**—the way the writer feels about his or her subject. When an author does not state his or her perspective directly, you need to look for clues. The author's word choice and tone (attitude) can reveal his or her perspective. The information that he or she chooses to include or leave out can provide clues as well.

Identifying Perspective As you read the article, "Canines to the Rescue," pay attention to how the author describes the events. What is the tone—admiring, critical, or something else? What words does the author use to describe the dogs? What information on the rescues does the author include in the article and what information does he leave out?

SELECTION VOCABULARY

arduous (AHR JOO UHS) *adj.:* difficult.
> *The crumbling building made finding the survivors an arduous task.*

persevered (PUR SUH VEERD) *v.:* kept trying; persisted.
> *Despite the difficulties, the dogs persevered in their search.*

fidelity (FUH DEHL UH TEE) *n.:* faithfulness.
> *The dogs showed true fidelity to their handlers by not giving up despite their discomfort.*

WORD STUDY

DIRECTIONS: When you find an unfamiliar word, look at the surrounding text for clues to figure out its meaning. These clues can be words that mean the same or the opposite of the unfamiliar word. Circle the words that provide clues to the meanings of *arduous* and *persevered* in the paragraph below.

> The dogs faced an *arduous* challenge. Finding buried survivors was very difficult. Yet the dogs refused to give up. They *persevered* until they had found five people in the rubble.

SKILLS FOCUS

Informational Text Skills
Analyze the author's perspective on a subject.

CANINES TO THE RESCUE

by Jonah Goldberg

> **BACKGROUND**
> The following article is about rescue dogs—dogs that are trained
> to save the lives of people in danger. Jonah Goldberg also looks
> at why these dogs help people and how the people who work
> with rescue dogs feel about them.

I spent the better part of an afternoon about half a mile south
of where the World Trade Center[1] stood, with Tara, a three-year-
old golden retriever employed by Michael Stanton Associates,
a private security firm. Tara's job is to find bombs. Of course,
she doesn't know that they are bombs; all she knows is that
her human master wants her to find something that smells
like plastic explosives, or TNT, or a dozen other dangerous
substances. The only payment she will receive for this is a few
moments fetching the ball with her boss.

10   This work ethic is the heart of canine exceptionalism. **A**
The dog is the only animal that volunteers for duty. If we want
other animals—horses, oxen, mules, falcons, bears, or parrots—to
come to our aid, we must either force them or bribe them. You
might even call horses our slaves: Their spirit must actually be
broken before they will agree to do anything for us. **B**

    Long before the rubble settled in downtown New York,
German shepherds, Labrador retrievers, and Rottweilers—as well
as canines of less aristocratic lineage—were already pulling at
their leashes to help with the search-and-rescue efforts. Locating
20 the dead and searching (too often in vain) for the living is
obviously an arduous and emotionally draining task for human
beings, but it is no picnic for dogs either. The rubble provided

---

1. **World Trade Center:** twin towers in New York City that were
destroyed on September 11, 2001.

From "Canines to the Rescue" by
Jonah Goldberg from *National Review*,
November 2001, pp. 34, 36. Copyright
© 2001 by National Review, Inc., 215
Lexington Avenue, New York, N.Y. 10016.
Reproduced by permission of **National
Review**.

A **LANGUAGE COACH**

What smaller word, or
root word, is the word
exceptionalism based on?
Look up the definition of
the root word in the dictionary and then write what you
think *exceptionalism* means.

_____

_____

B **READING FOCUS**

What is the author's
perspective on dogs here?

_____

_____

_____

A **VOCABULARY**

Selection Vocabulary
Underline the clues in this paragraph that help you understand the meaning of the word *arduous*.

B **READ AND DISCUSS**

Comprehension
How does this information add to what you know about rescue dogs?

unstable footing, was full of glass shards and twisted metal, and sometimes glowed red hot. Dangerous fumes, loud noises, and the equivalent of landslides were constant sources of distraction and peril. Dogs repeatedly had to limp out of the wreckage on bloody paws, the razor-edged debris[2] slicing through even the leather boots distributed to some of them. **A** **B**

30 Worse, the stress associated with not finding survivors was extreme; dogs tasked with this assignment expect—*need*—to find survivors. "They don't like to find bodies. They'll find them, but they don't feel rewarded," veterinarian Douglas Wyler explained. "The dogs are good, they're professionals, but like any professional they can suffer from melancholy and depression. It's hard for the men not to find anyone alive, and the dogs sense that."

But the dogs persevered. Consider Servus, a Belgian Malinois (a smaller version of the German shepherd) who arrived at the Twin Towers site with his owner, police officer Chris Christensen, the day after the disaster. While searching 40 for survivors, Servus fell down a nine-foot hole into a mound of dust and debris. When they pulled him free, "he couldn't breathe," Christensen explained. Servus tried to vomit, to no avail. By the time the convulsions started and Servus's tongue turned purple, between twenty and thirty men were gathered to help an animal they clearly considered a colleague (often, police dogs are given full-dress funerals). The canine was rushed to one of the veterinary MASH units set up to treat the rescue dogs as well as the numerous "civilian" animals and pets injured or abandoned in the surrounding residential areas.

50 The vets managed to resuscitate[3] Servus, and he was given an IV.[4] (It was not unusual to see rescue humans and rescue dogs lying beside one another, each with his own IV drip.) When the vets unstrapped the dog from the gurney and released him for

---

2. **debris** (DUH BREE): pieces of stone, wood, glass, or other materials left after something is destroyed.
3. **resuscitate** (RIH SUHS IH TAYT): revive; bring back to life.
4. **IV** (abbreviation for *intravenous*): medical procedure in which blood, plasma, medicine, or nutrients are delivered directly into a vein.

some doggie R&R,[5] he ran straight from the tent and leapt into the police car assigned to bring dogs to ground zero. "I couldn't believe it," Christensen said. "I told him three times to get out and he just looked at me, so we went to work. We worked for seven hours." **C**

C READ AND DISCUSS

Comprehension
What does this anecdote about Servus show us?

Such dedication has inspired a growing effort in the scientific community to explain this age-old symbiosis between men and dogs. Until fairly recently, the study of dogs has been ignored by scientists more interested in more "authentic" animals—despite the fact that the domestic dog may be the second most successful of all mammal species, after human beings.

More to the point, their success is directly attributable to the fact that they have teamed up with human beings. I'm told that according to an American Indian legend, human beings and animals were separated by a great canyon in prehistory. Forced to choose sides, the dog decided to throw in his lot with man and leapt the chasm to live and work with us. The moral of the story is certainly true, though the choice was evolutionary as well as sentimental. Some, like nature writer Stephen Budiansky, take the story too far in the other direction. He argues that canines have mastered an evolutionary strategy that makes us love them: "Dogs belong to that elite group of con artists at the very pinnacle of their profession, the ones who pick our pockets clean and leave us smiling about it."

---

5. **R&R**: abbreviation used in the military, meaning "rest and recuperation."

© Alan Diaz/AP Photos

A READ AND DISCUSS

Comprehension
What does this paragraph tell you about the author's view of dogs and their place in society?

B READING FOCUS

What is the author's **perspective** on rescue dogs?

_____

_____

_____

_____

© Alan Diaz/AP Photos

These cynics would have us believe that dogs—which have, in numerous documented cases, given their lives for human beings—are actually slyly exploiting an emotional glitch in people that makes us love soft, big-eyed furry things. This overlooks the obvious fact that we "con" dogs too; that they, in fact, love us as much as, if not more than, we love them.

Allowing himself to be carried by crane hundreds of feet above the ground and then lowered into a smoldering pit of metal and glass defies every instinct a dog has, except one: to be a selfless friend of his ally and master. "Histories are more full of examples of the fidelity of dogs than of friends," observed Alexander Pope. "Heaven goes by favor," remarked Mark Twain. "If it went by merit, you would stay out and your dog would go in." **A**

There's no disputing that dogs do things for canine reasons. Many of their heroic acts can be attributed to misplaced maternal or other instincts. Newfoundlands have saved many people from drowning, but their instinct is just as strong to "save" banana crates and other flotsam. Tara—the ebullient[6] golden retriever I looked for bombs with—doesn't know the details; all she knows is that she wants to please her human master.

And isn't that good enough? **B**

_____

6. **ebullient** (IH BUHL YUHNT): high-spirited.

Applying Your Skills

Canines to the Rescue

VOCABULARY DEVELOPMENT

DIRECTIONS: Write the letter of the word or phrase that most closely means the *opposite* of the vocabulary word. Two of the letters will not be used.

_____ **1.** arduous

_____ **2.** fidelity

_____ **3.** persevered

a. gave up

b. pressed on

c. easy

d. loyalty

e. unfaithful in nature

INFORMATIONAL TEXT FOCUS: ANALYZING AN AUTHOR'S PERSPECTIVE

DIRECTIONS: Fill out the following **perspective** wheel. Choose examples from "Canines to the Rescue" that tell about the author's tone and word choice, as well as the information related to the topic of the article that was included or not included.

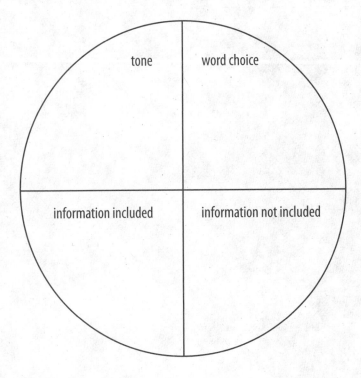

tone

word choice

information included

information not included

SKILLS FOCUS

Reading Skill
Analyze an author's perspective.

Skills Review

Collection 5

VOCABULARY REVIEW

DIRECTIONS: Match the vocabulary words below with their synonyms—the words or phrases that best match their meanings. Then, answer the question below.

_____	1. convey	a. complicated
_____	2. assured	b. impressive
_____	3. evident	c. communicate
_____	4. convoluted	d. foreign
_____	5. principal	e. clear
_____	6. arduous	f. unclear
_____	7. fidelity	g. difficult
_____	8. formidable	h. promised
_____	9. exotic	i. faithfulness
_____	10. ambiguous	j. most important

11. Which two vocabulary words have opposite meanings?

_____

Skills Review

Collection 5

LANGUAGE COACH

DIRECTIONS: A **suffix** is a word part added to the end of a word. One example is the suffix *–ity,* which means "having a particular quality." Identify the words in the Word Box on the previous page that use the *–ity* suffix. Use each word in a sentence below.

1. _____

2. _____

DIRECTIONS: The *–ity* ending can be added to other words on the vocabulary list as well. How does the meaning of *ambiguous* change when it becomes *ambiguity*? Look up the definition of each word. How has the meaning changed? How has it remained the same?

3. *ambiguity:* _____

4. *ambiguous:* _____

5. How do they compare? _____

6. *normal:* _____

7. *normality:* _____

8. How do they compare? _____

ORAL LANGUAGE ACTIVITY

DIRECTIONS: "Names/Nombres" and "Barrio Boy" deal with the experience of being a stranger in a new school. Write a brief speech that expresses your point of view about attending a new school for the first time. This could be a story about the very first day at school or your first experience at a new school after moving or changing grades. Organize your speech so that you include important examples or details that will make it easier for others to understand your experience. What did you like and dislike about the new school? Choose words and a speaking tone that best express the way you feel about your topic. Share your speech with a classmate or the entire class.

Reading for Life

Literary and Academic Vocabulary for Collection 6

sequence (SEE KWUHNS) *n.:* specific order in which things follow one another.
Technical directions arrange the steps you must follow in sequence.

technique (TEHK NEEK) *n.:* method of doing a particular task.
Her painting technique was very precise.

function (FUHNGK SHUHN) *n.:* purpose of a specific person or thing.
His function in the company was to give tours to the public.

communicate (KUH MYOO NUH KAYT) *v.:* share information or ideas.
When you are travelling, do you want to communicate by phone or email?

advertisements (AD VUHR TYZ MEHNTS) *n.:* public notices that tell you about consumer goods.
The advertisement said the hit movie had just been released on DVD.

labels (LAY BUHLZ) *n.:* printed information on a product that informs the consumer.
The labels on the soup cans listed ingredients and nutritional value.

memorandums (MEH MUH RAN DUHMZ) *n.:* brief written messages, also known as memos, often used to communicate within an office or business.
The company sent memorandums to all managers about the schedule change.

Casting Call

INFORMATIONAL TEXT FOCUS: PUBLIC DOCUMENTS

Public documents inform you of things you might need or want to know. These documents may be flyers or advertisements in newspapers or on the Internet. Public documents may be issued by schools, places of worship, government agencies, courts, libraries, and fire and police departments, just to name a few. Here are some tips for analyzing public documents:

- Important information may be set in boldfaced type.
- Some public documents contain a mix of fact and opinion.
- Pay careful attention when step-by-step instructions appear.

READING FOCUS: SKIMMING AND SCANNING

When you **skim**, you look at a selection quickly to see what it's about. When you **scan**, you look for information that is related to what you want to learn about. Before reading "Casting Call," skim the document to get the main ideas.

SELECTION VOCABULARY

charismatic (KAR IHZ MAT IHK) *adj.*: possessing energy, charm, or appeal.
> *The producers were looking for charismatic teens to play roles in the movie.*

WORD STUDY

DIRECTIONS: Write "Yes" after each sentence below if the vocabulary word is being used correctly. Write "No" if it is not.

1. It is helpful for a President of the United States to be **charismatic**. _____

2. After the ceremony, a **charismatic** will be served in the lobby. _____

3. The teacher was so **charismatic**, her students fell asleep. _____

SKILLS FOCUS

Informational Text Skills
Analyze a public document.

Reading Skills
Understand skimming and scanning.

CASTING CALL

If you've been looking for the right break to get into motion pictures, this may be your chance. Street-Wheelie Productions is casting fresh talent for an upcoming action movie.

To audition, you must

- be a charismatic, awesome, off-the-wall male or female individualist **A**
- be an expert at making your BMX-type bike do whatever you want it to do
- have your own bike

10
- look like you're between the ages of twelve and fifteen
- meet the requirements for a permit to work in the entertainment industry if you are under age eighteen
- be living in or near San Francisco during July and August 2004

Auditions will be held in
Golden Gate Park, San Francisco
Saturday, May 25, 2004
10:00 A.M. to 5:00 P.M.

Bring your bike.

See you in the movies! B

A **VOCABULARY**

Selection Vocabulary
The word *charismatic* means "possessing energy, charm or appeal." Rewrite this bullet point in your own words.

_____
_____
_____
_____

B **READING FOCUS**

Scan this **public document**. Which words are written in boldfaced type? Why do you think they are in boldface?

_____
_____
_____

Casting Call

USE A CONCEPT MAP

DIRECTIONS: Suppose that you are Sam's friend and you see the "Casting Call" flyer before she does. You decide to give only the most import information to Sam so she can audition. Use the skills you have practiced for analyzing public documents and skimming and scanning to complete the concept map below.

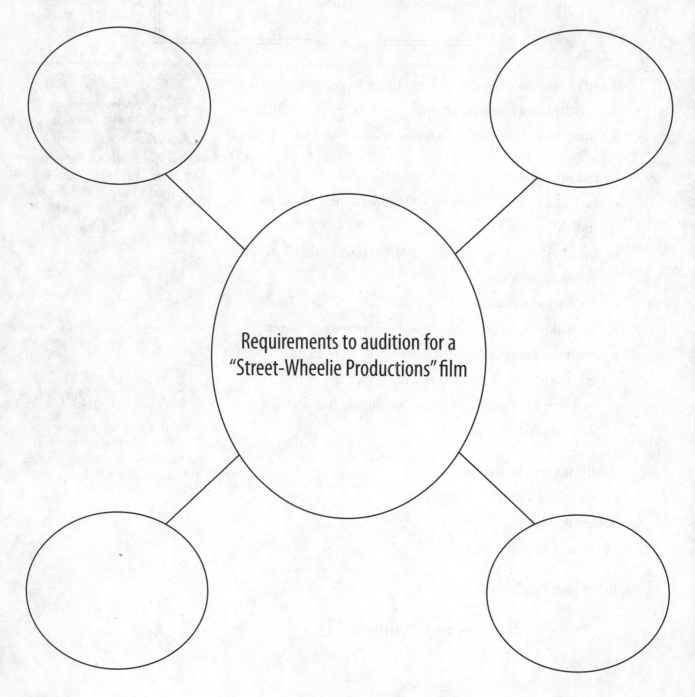

Requirements to audition for a "Street-Wheelie Productions" film

Applying Your Skills

Casting Call

VOCABULARY DEVELOPMENT

The adjective *charismatic* comes from the noun *charisma*, meaning "the quality of possessing energy, charm or appeal."

DIRECTIONS: Complete the exercises below by deciding whether *charismatic* or *charisma* better completes each sentence. Write your answers on the blank lines.

1. The candidate was so charming; he had a lot of _____.
2. The _____ leader got all of his people to support his plans.

INFORMATIONAL TEXT FOCUS: PUBLIC DOCUMENTS

DIRECTIONS: Review the tips for analyzing **public documents** given in the Preparing to Read section. Then complete the chart below to show which elements of a public document are used in "Casting Call." If an element is used, write a short example of where it is used.

Elements of a Public Document	Used in "Casting Call?"
Important information set in boldfaced type	1.
Information that mixes facts and opinions	2.
Step-by-step instructions	3.

READING FOCUS: SKIMMING AND SCANNING

DIRECTIONS: Imagine that you are a thirteen-year-old stunt bike rider living in San Francisco in 2004. Now **skim** and **scan** "Casting Call" with that mindset. What information in the document would be most important to you? Why?

_____

_____

Informational Text Skills
Understand the structure of public documents.

Reading Skills
Understand skimming and scanning.

Letter from Casting Director

INFORMATIONAL TEXT FOCUS: ANALYZING WORKPLACE DOCUMENTS

Whether you work in a small or large business, your working life will depend on many types of **workplace documents**. Businesses put important information in writing so that agreements, decisions, and requirements are clear to everyone involved. On the following pages, you will analyze a business letter.

READING FOCUS: PREVIEW THE TEXT

Before you read a workplace document, you should **preview the text** to find out what the document contains. This will help you decide whether the text is important to you or has useful information. When you preview, do not read every single word. Instead, look for elements such as titles, subheadings, charts, graphs, photos, and captions.

Use the Skill   Preview "Letter from Casting Director." Without reading the entire letter, make predictions about the type of information it will contain based on clues in the text.

SELECTION VOCABULARY

punctuality (PUHNGK CHU AL UH TEE) *n.:* quality of being on time.
   The actors' punctuality will help keep the production on schedule.

WORD STUDY

DIRECTIONS: *Punctuality* is formed from the adjective *punctual*, which means "on time." Some of the words listed below are synonyms of *punctual* and *punctuality*. Synonyms are words that have similar meanings. Write "yes" next to the word if it is a synonym of *punctual* or *punctuality*. Write "no" if it is not.

_____ **1.** late

_____ **2.** dependable

_____ **3.** promptness

_____ **4.** slow

_____ **5.** quickness

_____ **6.** prompt

SKILLS FOCUS

Informational Text Skills
Analyze a workplace document.

Reading Skills
Preview text.

LETTER FROM CASTING DIRECTOR

BACKGROUND
Sam's audition has gone really well. Everyone is as nice as can be, and someone takes down all of Sam's information and talks with her and her mother for quite a while. Pretty soon, Sam receives the business letter below.

Letter from Casting Director

STREET WHEELIE PRODUCTIONS

2323 South Robertson Boulevard
Beverly Hills, CA 90210

June 7, 2004

Miss Samantha Lancaster

1920 Ygnacio Valley Road

Walnut Creek, CA 94598 **A**

Dear Sam:

10 It is my pleasure to offer you a part in our production. Attached is your contract. The items in the contract spell out the issues we discussed last Saturday, as follows:

- You are responsible for your own transportation to and from filming.
- Check your e-mail first thing each morning and last thing each night. **B**
- Report to makeup, hair, and wardrobe two hours before your first call.
- Report with your bike for all calls. You may not wash or
20 otherwise clean all that great grunge off your bike.
- Because you are not yet age sixteen, a parent or guardian must be present whenever you are working. As we discussed

A **READING FOCUS**

As you **preview** this letter, what does this heading information tell you?

_____

_____

_____

B **READING FOCUS**

How does the use of bullet points help you **preview** the letter?

_____

_____

_____

A READ AND DISCUSS

Comprehension

What is the purpose of this letter?

B VOCABULARY

Selection Vocabulary

Circle all of the instructions in this letter that have to do with *punctuality*.

C READING FOCUS

What qualities make this a **workplace document**?

_____

_____

_____

_____

with your mother, your grandfather will be an appropriate guardian.

- Nonprofessional actors are paid a minimum hourly wage. Your eight-hour-maximum workday will begin when you arrive each day and end when you leave each day. By law you may not work more than eight hours a day. One paid hour of rest and recreation will be part of your eight-hour workday,

30   but the thirty-minute lunch, also paid, will *not* be part of the workday. You will always have twelve hours or more between the end of one workday and the makeup call for the next. **A**

- You will receive a bonus at the end of your filming schedule. This bonus will be paid on your last day of work, on the condition that you have fulfilled all aspects of your contract with regard to attendance, punctuality, and appearance. **B** This bonus will equal the total of all your previous hourly checks.

If you have any questions, call Juanita Diaz, our lawyer. Her phone number is on the contract. We look forward to having

40   you on the project.

Sincerely,

Cassandra Rice

Cassandra Rice, Casting Director **C**

Applying Your Skills

Letter from Casting Director

VOCABULARY DEVELOPMENT

DIRECTIONS: Circle any of the following sentences that correctly use the word *punctuality*. Cross out sentences that use the word incorrectly.

1. Because of her *punctuality*, we had to delay starting the movie until the next day.

2. I appreciated his *punctuality* because it meant we could start filming on time.

3. She followed the correct *punctuality* that was asked of her.

INFORMATIONAL TEXT FOCUS: ANALYZING WORKPLACE DOCUMENTS

DIRECTIONS: Suppose you are the one who received the letter from the casting director. You call a friend to tell her only the most important information in the letter. If you only had time to tell her three things from the letter, which pieces of information would you choose? Write them below.

1. _____

_____

2. _____

_____

3. _____

_____

READING FOCUS: PREVIEW THE TEXT

DIRECTIONS: Copy the Venn diagram below onto a separate sheet of paper and complete it by comparing the predictions you made when you **previewed** "Letter from Casting Director" with the actual information it contains.

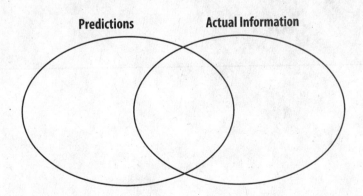

Predictions   Actual Information

SKILLS FOCUS

Informational Skills
Analyze a workplace document.

Reading Skills
Preview text.

BART System Map

INFORMATIONAL TEXT FOCUS: CONSUMER DOCUMENTS

A consumer buys what someone else sells. For example, if you buy an ice cream cone, you are a consumer. Sometimes, consumers need information about the products and services they buy. **Consumer documents** provide that information. On the following pages, you will analyze a consumer document.

READING FOCUS: UNDERSTAND GRAPHIC AIDS

Many consumer documents use **graphic aids.** These include maps, graphs, tables, and illustrations. You should look at the titles of these graphics to see if they might contain information you need.

Maps are drawings of land areas. They can show things like mountains or country borders. The map you will read shows train routes. Maps usually give you information to help you understand what is being shown. There may be a scale to explain distances, a **key** to explain the symbols on the map, and a compass rose to show directions. Pay attention to the labels on the map and what the different colors represent.

As you read the "BART System Map," make a list of the features that help you to read the map. Use a **table** like this one.

Map Feature	How it is helpful

BART SYSTEM MAP

Consumer Documents

Read with a Purpose Read these **consumer documents** to learn how Sam locates the information she needs to get to work.

Locating Information: Transit Map

Sam has to travel from Walnut Creek to the movie set location and back with her bike, and her grandfather has to go with her. The two decide to take the Bay Area Rapid Transit System, better known as BART. BART is a network of trains that can take you just about anywhere in the San Francisco Bay Area. First, Sam and her grandfather log on to the Internet to look at the **BART system map.** They want to be sure they can get from their home in Walnut Creek to the Embarcadero Station, where the StreetWheelie production van will be waiting. They find the map that is shown on the next page.

© Stockbyte Platinum/Alamy

A **VOCABULARY**

Academic Vocabulary
What is the **function**, or purpose, of this Web site?

File   Edit   View   Favorites   Tools   Help

Back   Forward   Stop   Refresh   Home   Search   Favorites   History   Mail   Print

Address   http://www.bart.gov/   Go

San Francisco Bay Area Rapid Transit District

BART

Site Map | Contact Us | Search BART   GO

Stations & Schedules | Tickets | Rider Guide | News | About BART | Home

Welcome to BART

606 Unit 3 · Collection 6

A

Word Study

BART is an acronym. Acronyms are words formed by combining the first letters of a series of words. Find another acronym on this map. Write the acronym and what it stands for on the lines below.

_____

_____

_____

_____

B **READING FOCUS**

Study the **map key** carefully. How can you tell the different rail lines apart?

_____

_____

_____

C **READING FOCUS**

What makes the BART system map a **consumer document**? (Think about who it is made for and how it is used.)

_____

_____

_____

_____

D **READ AND DISCUSS**

Comprehension

What has Sam learned from the BART System Map?

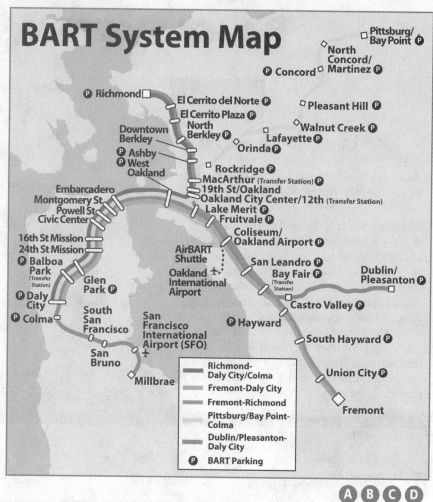

BART System Map

Pittsburg/Bay Point ℗

North Concord/Martinez ◇

℗ Concord

□ Pleasant Hill ℗

℗ Richmond □

El Cerrito del Norte ℗

El Cerrito Plaza ℗

Walnut Creek ℗

Downtown Berkley

North Berkley ℗

Lafayette ℗

℗ Ashby

Orinda ℗

℗ West Oakland

□ Rockridge ℗

MacArthur (Transfer Station) ℗

Embarcadero

19th St/Oakland

Montgomery St

Oakland City Center/12th (Transfer Station)

Powell St

Civic Center

Lake Merit ℗

Fruitvale ℗

16th St Mission

Coliseum/ Oakland Airport ℗

24th St Mission

AirBART Shuttle

San Leandro ℗

℗ Balboa Park (Transfer Station)

Bay Fair (Transfer Station) ℗

Dublin/ Pleasanton ℗

Glen Park ℗

Oakland International Airport ✈

Castro Valley ℗

℗ Daly City

South San Francisco

San Francisco International Airport (SFO)

℗ Hayward

South Hayward ℗

℗ Colma

San Bruno

✈

Union City ℗

◇ Millbrae

Fremont ◇

▬	Richmond-Daly City/Colma
▬	Fremont-Daly City
▬	Fremont-Richmond
▬	Pittsburg/Bay Point-Colma
▬	Dublin/Pleasanton-Daly City
℗	BART Parking

A B C D

🌐 Internet

Applying Your Skills

BART System Map

INFORMATIONAL TEXT FOCUS: CONSUMER DOCUMENTS

DIRECTIONS: Answer the following questions about the **consumer document** you just read:

1. Which BART line stops at Walnut Creek?

_____

_____

2. Which stops have parking along the Richmond-Daly City/Colma line?

_____

_____

3. Name two transfer stations shown on the map.

_____

_____

4. What other information about the BART system can Sam find on this Web site?

_____

_____

READING FOCUS: UNDERSTAND GRAPHIC AIDS

DIRECTIONS: Look back at the list of features you made while reading. Use the information you gathered to complete the **table** below.

Map feature	How it is helpful
1. Each train line has its own color.	
2. The name of each train line is shown in a key.	
3. Each train stop is shown with a white bar and a label.	
4. Land and water areas are shown in different colors.	

SKILLS FOCUS

Informational Text Skills
Analyze a consumer document by reading a map.

Reading Skills
Understand graphic aids on a map.

How to Change a Flat Tire

INFORMATIONAL TEXT FOCUS: ANALYZING TECHNICAL DIRECTIONS

Technical directions are step-by-step instructions that explain how to complete mechanical tasks. For example, you may follow technical directions when you assemble a video game system. On the following pages, you will analyze directions that explain how to change a flat tire on a car.

READING FOCUS: PREVIEWING THE TEXT

Some technical directions seem overwhelming because they contain so much information. **Previewing the text** can help you find only the important information you need. Preview a text by looking at headings, lists, and tables without reading every word.

SELECTION VOCABULARY

procedures (PRUH SEE JUHRZ) *n.:* methods of doing things.

The proper procedures for changing a flat tire are given in the directions.

standard (STAN DUHRD) *adj.:* usual; regularly used or produced.

If you have a standard transmission, put your car in gear.

WORD STUDY

DIRECTIONS: Sometimes you can understand the meaning of an unfamiliar word by looking for clues about what it does *not* mean. In the following sentence, underline clues that mean the opposite of the vocabulary word.

We need a *standard* part for this car, not something unique that you only make here.

SKILLS FOCUS

Informational Text Skills
Analyze technical directions.

Reading Skills
Preview a text.

How to Change a Flat Tire A

Read with a Purpose
Read these instructions to learn how to change a flat tire.

Before you can change a flat tire on your car, you first have to realize that the tire is flat. You might come out of your house in the morning and see the wheel rim resting on the road with the tire spread around it. You'll know right away that the tire's flat. How can you tell, though, if it goes flat while you are driving? A first clue is that your car starts to pull to the right or the left even though you aren't turning the steering wheel. Another clue is that passing motorists honk and point as they drive by. Yet another clue is that the car starts bouncing up and down and making a loud *thumpity-thump-thump* sound. **B**

When you suspect you have a flat tire, follow these procedures:

STEP 1

Park the car as far off the road as possible. Put the car in park (if you have an automatic transmission) or in gear (if you have a standard transmission), turn off the engine, and put on the emergency **C** brake. Turn on your car's flashing lights. Now, get out and look at your tires. If you have a flat, put out emergency triangles or, at night, flares. (It's a good idea to carry warning triangles and flares in your trunk at all times in case of an emergency.)

Vocabulary **procedures** (pruh SEE juhrz) *n.*: methods of doing things.
standard (STAN duhrd) *adj.*: usual; regularly used or produced.

A **READING FOCUS**

Preview the text. What elements should you look at briefly in order to get an idea of what you are about to learn?

_____

_____

_____

B **VOCABULARY**

Word Study

The word *thump* is an example of onomatopoeia. This is a word that imitates the sound it is referencing. What other example of onomatopoeia can you think of?

_____

_____

C **VOCABULARY**

Selection Vocabulary

Standard can mean "usual." It can also mean "a type of flag." Which meaning of *standard* is being used here?

_____

_____

Academic Vocabulary

The directions are listed in *sequence*, or in order. How can you tell each step in the sequence apart?

_____

_____

B **READING FOCUS**

It is important that you check your understanding of **technical directions**. Rewrite this step using your own words.

_____

_____

_____

C **READ AND DISCUSS**

Comprehension

What do the steps illustrating the way to change a tire show you about the process?

STEP 2 Remove the spare tire from the trunk. Also take out the jack, the lug wrench, and related tools.

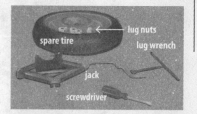
spare tire · lug nuts · lug wrench · jack · screwdriver

STEP 3 Remove the wheel cover from the flat tire, using a screwdriver or the end of the jack handle. **A**

STEP 4 Loosen the lug nuts with the lug wrench, but do not remove them. Most lug nuts turn counterclockwise.

STEP 5 Position your jack. Different makes of cars come with different types of jacks, so check your owner's manual to learn how to use your jack. Make sure the jack is sitting on a solid, flat surface. **B**

STEP 6 Lift the car with the jack until your flat tire is two or three inches off the ground. *(Never lie under the car when it is on the jack!)* **C**

STEP 7
Now, finish unscrewing the lug nuts. Put them inside the wheel cover so you don't lose them.

STEP 8
Remove the flat tire, and replace it with the spare tire. Replace the lug nuts, and tighten them by hand.

STEP 9
Lower the jack until the spare tire is firmly on the ground. Remove the jack. Firmly tighten the lug nuts with the lug wrench. Work diagonally—tighten one on the top, then one on the bottom; one on the left, then one on the right; and so on.

STEP 10
Place the flat tire, the wheel cover, and all your tools in the trunk. As soon as you can, drive to a garage or a tire repair shop to get the tire fixed or replaced. You never want to be without a spare, because you never know when you'll get another flat!

D · LANGUAGE COACH

The word *cover* has **multiple meanings.** Which meaning is being used here?

_____

_____

_____

How to Change a Flat Tire

USE A SEQUENCE CHART

DIRECTIONS: The steps from "How to Change a Flat Tire" are in the sequence chart below, but they are out of order! Place them in order by writing the correct step number before each direction.

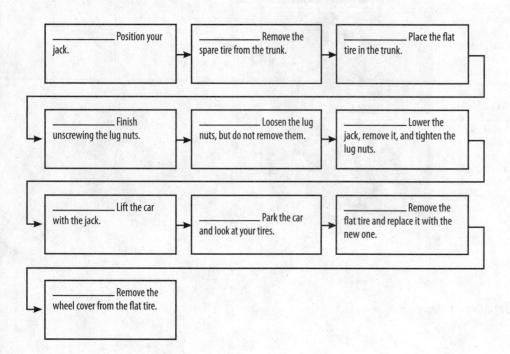

_____ Position your jack.

_____ Remove the spare tire from the trunk.

_____ Place the flat tire in the trunk.

_____ Finish unscrewing the lug nuts.

_____ Loosen the lug nuts, but do not remove them.

_____ Lower the jack, remove it, and tighten the lug nuts.

_____ Lift the car with the jack.

_____ Park the car and look at your tires.

_____ Remove the flat tire and replace it with the new one.

_____ Remove the wheel cover from the flat tire.

Applying Your Skills

How to Change a Flat Tire

VOCABULARY DEVELOPMENT

DIRECTIONS: Complete the paragraph by filling in the correct vocabulary words from the Word Box.

Word Box

procedures

standard

Manuals often include (1) _____ for repairing or replacing parts. You must do these in the correct sequence. It is also important that these parts use (2) _____ sizes so that they will fit.

INFORMATIONAL TEXT FOCUS: ANALYZING TECHNICAL DIRECTIONS

DIRECTIONS: Analyze **technical directions** by answering the questions below.

1. Why can't you leave out the step of putting the car in park after you pull over to the side of the road?

   _____

   _____

2. What is the purpose of the pictures that follow each step?

   _____

   _____

3. Why do you think the directions warn you never to lie under the car when it is on the jack?

   _____

   _____

READING FOCUS: PREVIEWING THE TEXT

DIRECTIONS: Answer the following questions based on what you learned from **previewing** "How to Change a Flat Tire."

1. Which step tells you where to put your lug nuts? _____

2. What is the second step? _____

3. What do you do before you start working on removing your flat?

   _____

4. What step tells you how to position a jack? _____

5. What is the final step? _____

Informational Text Skills
Analyze technical directions.

Reading Skills
Preview the text.

Tilting at Windmills: The Search for Alternative Energy Sources

INFORMATIONAL TEXT FOCUS: CAUSE AND EFFECT

You know from experience that one thing leads to another. If you sleep through your alarm, you know you'll be late for school. Sleeping through your alarm is a **cause**—it makes something happen. An **effect** is what happens as a result of some event—in this case, you're late for school.

When you read a text and ask yourself, "Why did this happen?" and "What happened because of this?" you are asking about causes and effects. As you read the article, keep track of causes and effects with a chart like this one:

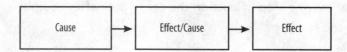

SELECTION VOCABULARY

shortages (SHAWR TIHJ IHZ) *n.:* situations in which needed items cannot be gotten in sufficient amounts.
There were shortages of oil in the 1970s.

WORD STUDY

DIRECTIONS: Writers sometimes provide the definition to an unfamiliar word in the text. Often this definition will be in the same sentence as the unfamiliar word. Look at the following sentence and underline the word or words that define the vocabulary word.

1. There are often *shortages* during wartime, and many people suffer from malnutrition because of the lack of food.

SKILLS FOCUS

Informational Text Skills
Identify causes and effects in the text.

TILTING AT WINDMILLS: THE SEARCH FOR ALTERNATIVE ENERGY RESOURCES

> **BACKGROUND**
> For many years now, scientists have been studying sources of energy other than fossil fuels (coal, oil, and natural gas), which will run out one day. Alternative energy resources include hydro-electric (running water), solar (the sun), and wind power. Each of these power sources has advantages and disadvantages. This article examines efforts to use the wind to generate power.

When you turn on a light, a television, or a computer, you probably don't give much thought to how the electricity powering those devices got there. But fuel was used to create that electrical charge. And chances are, it was a fossil fuel, gotten from decaying plants and animals.

Over millions of years, dead plants and animals get buried and then turn into substances like coal, oil, and natural gas. These products are found in underground deposits that are mined by energy companies. Fossil fuels are natural,
10 in a sense, but using them can create some nasty by-products. Coal and the like are burned to release their energy, and the burning fuel releases harmful substances called emissions into the atmosphere. **A**

In addition to the problem of causing pollution, fossil fuels are also running out. There is a limited supply of fossil fuel in the ground, and because it takes millions of years to form, it is considered a nonrenewable energy source. So power companies are increasingly turning to an alternative source of energy: the wind. "Strong growth figures in the U.S. prove that wind
20 is now a mainstream option for new power generation," said

A VOCABULARY

Word Study
Look up the definition of *by-products* in a dictionary and write it in the lines below. Then, underline an example of *by-products* in this paragraph.

_____

_____

_____

A READ AND DISCUSS

Comprehension
What's the problem with fossil fuels?

B READ AND DISCUSS

Comprehension
What do you learn about the windmills?

C READING FOCUS

What is one **cause** of the windmill's popularity in the Netherlands? What **effect** has this had on the appearance of windmills?

_____

_____

_____

_____

Randy Swisher. He is president of the American Wind Energy Association. **A**

As Old as the Wind

Wind is the fastest-growing source of renewable energy, according to the United States Department of Energy. A renewable power source, such as wind or solar power, does not depend on a limited fuel supply. Wind is freely available and is used to generate power in more than thirty states. It keeps more than two million households running.

30   People first used wind to generate power around five thousand years ago. They used it to propel sailboats up and down the Nile River. Sometime between 500 and 900 A.D., the Persians realized that wind could be used to turn a wheel. They attached several sails to a central axle, and the windmill was born.

    Early windmills were used to pump water and grind grain, and many are still used for these tasks today. In the Netherlands, flooding is common, and farmers often need to move large amounts of water. Windmills are a workable solution. Because they are part of everyday life in the Netherlands, people have

40 tried to make these hardworking machines attractive. The country has become famous for its beautiful windmills, which dot the landscape. **B** **C**

© Adrian Buck/Alamy

Running with the Wind

The most widespread use of modern windmills is for creating electricity. Generating electricity requires a turbine, which is a kind of engine. Steam, water, air, or some other force turns a wheel or a set of wheels, which turns a shaft. This shaft usually turns a generator, which produces electricity.

Beginning in the 1920s, wind was used in a limited way to generate electricity in rural areas of the United States. Then came the energy crisis of the 1970s. Around the world, there were shortages of oil. The cost of fossil fuels soared. Because of these difficulties, interest in generating power from wind on a large scale grew. **D**

Giant "wind farms" were built in remote areas, where wind sweeps across the landscape. Other wind farms were built offshore, to capture sea breezes.

"As security of energy supply and climate change are ranging high on the political agendas of the world's governments, wind energy has already become a mainstream energy source in many countries around the world," said Arthouros Zervos. He is the chairman of the Global Wind Energy Council. "Wind energy is clean and fuel-free, which makes it the most attractive solution to the world's energy challenges."

Two gigantic wind farms are located off the coast of Denmark. Wind supplies 20 percent of Denmark's power. The United States ranks third, behind Germany and Spain, in the amount of power it generates from the wind. **E**

Facing the Wind

Wind farms are quite a sight. A typical power-generating windmill is enormous. It is around twenty stories tall, and the diameter of its blades is about 200 feet across. The taller the windmill and the longer its blades, the more wind it can capture. **F**

But giant wind farms are not always welcome. Some groups complain that wind farms spoil the landscape—or seascape. The

D VOCABULARY

Selection Vocabulary
When there is a *shortage* there is not enough of something. What happened as a result of the energy crisis of the 1970s?

_____

_____

_____

E READ AND DISCUSS

Comprehension
What is your response to this statement?

F READING FOCUS

What **effect** does having longer blades and being taller have on a windmill's function?

_____

_____

_____

© Steve Hamblin/Alamy

construction of a wind farm planned for an area near Cape Cod, Massachusetts, has been delayed because many people say it will ruin their view of the Atlantic Ocean. Large windmills can also be harmful to birds and other wildlife. And because wind is not constant, other power sources must be used when the wind is
80   not blowing.

Government programs, however, especially in the United States and Europe, are encouraging the use of wind power as an alternative to fossil fuels. This ancient technology can help us meet our energy needs without using up our natural resources and polluting the atmosphere. **A**

Applying Your Skills

Tilting at Windmills: The Search for Alternative Energy Sources

VOCABULARY DEVELOPMENT

DIRECTIONS: Knowing synonyms (words that mean the same thing) and antonyms (words that mean the opposite) can help you understand words. Write a synonym and an antonym for the word *shortage*.

Shortage:

1. synonym _____

2. antonym _____

INFORMATIONAL TEXT FOCUS: CAUSE AND EFFECT

DIRECTIONS: Fill in the missing **causes** and **effects** from the article in the chart below.

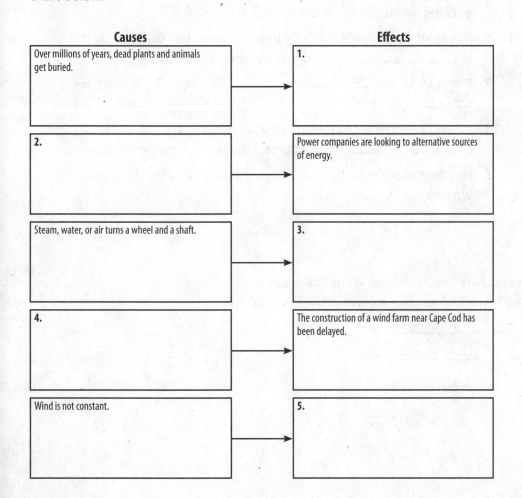

Causes	Effects
Over millions of years, dead plants and animals get buried.	1.
2.	Power companies are looking to alternative sources of energy.
Steam, water, or air turns a wheel and a shaft.	3.
4.	The construction of a wind farm near Cape Cod has been delayed.
Wind is not constant.	5.

SKILLS FOCUS

Reading Skill
Identify causes and effects in a text.

Collection 6

VOCABULARY REVIEW

DIRECTIONS: Fill in the blanks with the vocabulary words from the Word Box that best complete each sentence.

Word Box

communicate

function

procedures

punctuality

charismatic

sequence

shortages

standard

technique

1. Professor Smith was so _____ that all the students wanted to take his physics class.

2. She was known for her _____, and had never been late for work in her life.

3. Public documents try to _____ important facts to the public.

4. You must carry out steps in the correct _____ to get the desired result.

5. We followed the proper _____ for exiting the building when the fire alarm went off.

6. If are not sure what a part of a machine does, you can look up its _____ in an instructional manual.

7. When there are _____ of something, the price charged for it often rises.

8. When I buy a new car, I want one that has only the _____ features; I don't need anything extra.

9. He came up with a new _____ for making an omelette.

DIRECTIONS: Which of the vocabulary words in the Word Box mean the opposite of the words listed below? Write your answer in the space provided.

1. unique _____

2. abundance _____

3. delay _____

Collection 6

LANGUAGE COACH

DIRECTIONS: A **prefix** is a word part added to the beginning of a word to change its meaning. A **suffix** is a word part added to the end of a word to change its meaning. A suffix may also change a word's part of speech. Complete the activities below. Use a dictionary if you need help.

Some of the vocabulary words in the Word Box on the previous page already have suffixes attached. Look at the words below. What words do you end up with when you remove their suffixes?

1. charismatic _____

2. punctuality _____

Add a prefix or a suffix to each of the following words to create a different word. Write each word and its definition on the lines below.

3. standard _____

4. function _____

WRITING ACTIVITY

When you read nonfiction sources, it is important to look for balance in the argument that the writer makes. A balanced article gives information about more than one point of view on the topic.

DIRECTIONS: Does the writer of "Tilting at Windmills" provide a balanced view of the topic? Write three or four sentences that explain why you think the writer does or does not present a balanced view on using windmills to produce power.

Elements of Poetry

© Elly Godfroy/Alamy

Literary and Academic Vocabulary for Collection 7

vision (VIHZH UHN) *n.:* a mental image; force or power of imagination.
The theme of the poem reflects the poet's vision.

structure (STRUHK CHUHR) *n.:* the way in which a set of parts is put together to form a whole; organization.
To understand the structure of a poem you must look at its parts.

tradition (TRUH DIHSH UHN) *n.:* a set of beliefs or customs that have been handed down for generations.
Poetic traditions go back to the ancient world.

comment (KAHM EHNT) *v.:* to explain or interpret something.
Some poets comment on the relationship between people and nature.

tone (TOHN) *n.:* the attitude toward a subject.
When writing about a happy subject, the poet might choose a cheerful tone.

simile (SIHM UH LEE) *n.:* a comparison of two unlike things using the words *like* or *as.*
I used this simile in my poem: "The black horse moved like a shadow."

metaphor (MEHT UH FAWR) *n.:* a comparison of two unlike things that does not use *like* or *as.*
I used this metaphor in my story: "The horse was a black shadow."

I'm Nobody!

by Emily Dickinson

LITERARY FOCUS: FIGURES OF SPEECH AND EXTENDED METAPHOR

Writer Emily Dickinson highlights her ideas by using **figures of speech**. Figures of speech compare things that seem very different at first. By making unusual comparisons, the writer allows you to see familiar things in a new light. Comparisons in figures of speech are very imaginative and are not supposed to be taken literally.

The most common figures of speech are similes and metaphors. A **simile** compares two unlike things by using the words *like* or *as*. A **metaphor** directly compares two things without using *like* or *as*. See the chart below for examples of each.

Similes	Metaphors
The track star ran *like* a speeding bullet.	The track star was a bullet, speeding past the other racers.
Our neighbor's St. Bernard is *as* big *as* an elephant.	Our neighbor's St. Bernard is an elephant.
The idea rumbled through my mind *like* a freight train.	The idea was a freight train rumbling through my mind.

SKILLS FOCUS

Literary Skills
Understand figures of speech.

An **extended metaphor** is a metaphor that is developed for several lines rather than just one. Sometimes Dickinson will even draw an extended metaphor out over an entire poem. "I'm Nobody!" is only eight lines long, but as you read it, check to see for how many lines are used to develop the comparisons.

I'm Nobody

READING FOCUS: QUESTIONING THE TEXT

One way to better understand poetry—especially Emily Dickinson's poems, which can be complex and confusing—is to pause and **ask questions** from time to time. Sometimes you may ask a question, then immediately see its answer. Other times, you'll have to write your questions down and review them when you complete the poem.

Below are some lines from "I'm Nobody!" and examples of questions that you may ask while reading.

Line 1: "I'm Nobody! Who are you?"

My question: To whom is the poet speaking?

Line 4: "Don't tell! they'd banish us, you know!"

My question: Who is the poet referring to now, and why would anyone be banished (forced to leave a place)?

SKILLS FOCUS

Reading Skills
Ask questions to better understand a poem.

I'M NOBODY!

by Emily Dickinson

I'm Nobody! Who are you?
Are you Nobody too?
Then there's a pair of us!
Don't tell! they'd banish us, you know! **A**

5   How dreary to be Somebody!
How public—like a Frog—
To tell your name the livelong June
To an admiring Bog! **B** **C**

Senecio 1922 by Paul Klee. Oil on gauze on cardboard (40.5 x 38 cm). Oeffentliche Kunstsammlung Basel, Kunstmuseum. Accession no. 1569. © 2003 Artists Rights Society (ARS), New York/VG Bild–Kunst, Bonn

Applying Your Skills

I'm Nobody!

LITERARY FOCUS: FIGURES OF SPEECH AND EXTENDED METAPHOR

DIRECTIONS: Decide whether each of the following statements is true or false. If a statement is false, explain why.

1. When Dickinson insists that she's "Nobody," she's using a metaphor to explain that she prefers private life to public life.

   _____

2. The line "Don't tell! they'd banish us, you know!" is an example of a simile.

   _____

3. The idea of the "admiring Bog" is an extended metaphor.

   _____

READING FOCUS: QUESTIONING THE TEXT

DIRECTIONS: On the chart below, write three questions that you asked while reading "I'm Nobody!" Then, in the second column, attempt to answer your questions.

My Questions	Answers
1.	2.
3.	4.
5.	6.

SKILLS FOCUS

Literary Skills
Analyze figures of speech.

Reading Skills
Ask questions to improve your understanding of a poem.

The Runaway

by Robert Frost

LITERARY FOCUS: RHYME AND RHYME SCHEME

In a poem, words that **rhyme**, or have the same end sound, often come at the end of lines. These **end rhymes** determine the **rhyme scheme**, or pattern of rhymes, in a poem or section of a poem. Assign a different letter to each new end rhyme to identify the rhyme scheme of a poem. For example, if every other line has an end rhyme, then the rhyme scheme would begin *abab*. The *a*'s rhyme with each other and the *b*'s rhyme with each other.

Find Rhymes   As you read Robert Frost's poem "The Runaway," look for the end rhymes. Identify the rhyme scheme of the poem and write out the pattern using letters (*a*, *b*, *c* . . .).

Use the Skill   Look at the lines from Frost's poem. Write a letter next to each line to show the rhyme scheme of following "The Runaway:"

Once when the snow of the year was beginning to fall, _____

We stopped by a mountain pasture to say, "Whose colt?" _____

A little Morgan had one forefoot on the wall, _____

The other curled at his breast. He dipped his head _____

And snorted at us. And then he had to bolt. _____

We heard the miniature thunder where he fled, _____

And we saw him, or thought we saw him, dim and gray, _____

Like a shadow against the curtain of falling flakes. _____

SKILLS FOCUS

Literary Skills
Identify and understand rhymes and rhyme schemes.

Reading Skills
Read a poem by paying careful attention to punctuation.

The Runaway

READING SKILLS: READING A POEM

Robert Frost writes in a conversational tone. Use a similar tone as you read his poem aloud. To help you understand his poem, pay close attention to punctuation as you read. Follow these tips:

- Don't stop reading at the end of a line of poetry unless you see punctuation. Often poets continue an idea from one line to the next.

- Make a full stop for a period.

- Pause briefly at a comma, colon, semicolon, or dash.

- If a poem has no punctuation, do your best to figure out where to pause based on the thoughts expressed in the poem.

These tips will also help you read a poem out loud with the proper rhythm and pacing.

Use the Skill First, read "The Runaway" silently. Then, read it aloud, paying close attention to the punctuation tips above. Does the tone change when you read it aloud?

THE RUNAWAY

by Robert Frost

BACKGROUND
Robert Frost was one of America's most celebrated poets. He lived most of his life on farms in Vermont and New Hampshire. Many of his poems are filled with images from the farms and countryside of New England. His poem "The Runaway" is about a breed of horse called a Morgan. Morgans are fast and strong. The horse in the poem is only a colt—a young, male horse.

 LANGUAGE COACH

Dialogue is a conversation. In the poem you can find dialogue in quotation marks. Underline the dialogue in the first 14 lines of the poem.

 VOCABULARY

Academic Vocabulary

Try to form a *vision*, an image in your mind, of the horse's actions. What do you see?

_____

_____

_____

_____

_____

_____

_____

Once when the snow of the year was beginning to fall,

We stopped by a mountain pasture to say, "Whose colt?"

A little Morgan had one forefoot on the wall,

The other curled at his breast. He dipped his head

5   And snorted at us. And then he had to bolt.

We heard the miniature thunder where he fled,

And we saw him, or thought we saw him, dim and gray,

Like a shadow against the curtain of falling flakes.

"I think the little fellow's afraid of the snow.

10   He isn't winter-broken.[1] It isn't play

With the little fellow at all. He's running away.

I doubt if even his mother could tell him, 'Sakes,

It's only weather.' He'd think she didn't know!

Where is his mother? He can't be out alone."

15   And now he comes again with clatter of stone,

And mounts the wall again with whited eyes

And all his tail that isn't hair up straight.

He shudders his coat as if to throw off flies.

---

1. **winter-broken:** used to winter; to break a colt is to get a young horse used to being ridden.

"The Runaway" from *The Poetry of Robert Frost,* edited by Edward Connery Lathem. Copyright 1923, © 1969 by Henry Holt and Company; copyright © 1951 by Robert Frost. Reproduced by **Henry Holt and Company, LLC.**

© Bruce Dale/Getty Images

C **READING FOCUS**

Read the last four lines again. After which words do you pause? After which words do you stop? How do you know?

_____

_____

_____

_____

D **LITERARY FOCUS**

What is the **rhyme scheme** of these last three lines?

_____

_____

E **READ AND DISCUSS**

Comprehension
What is happening in this part?

"Whoever it is that leaves him out so late,

20   When other creatures have gone to stall and bin,

Ought to be told to come and take him in." C D E

The Runaway

USE A CHAIN OF EVENTS CHART

DIRECTIONS: Even in a short piece of writing such as the poem "The Runaway," writers often tell the events in sequence, or in order. These events build upon each other until they reach the conclusion of the story. Use a chain of events chart like the one below to record the main events in the poem in the correct order.

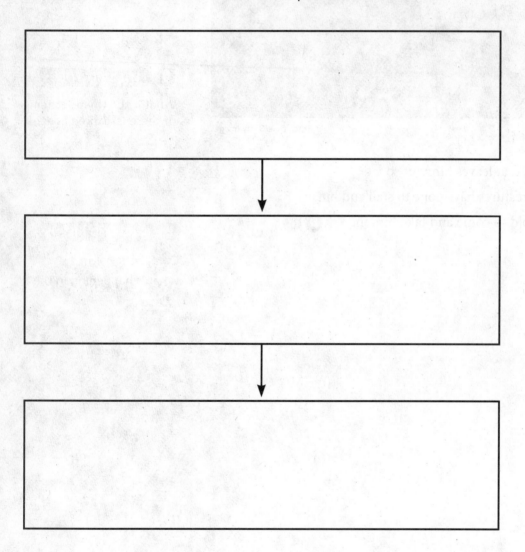

Applying Your Skills

The Runaway

LITERARY FOCUS: RHYME AND RHYME SCHEME

DIRECTIONS: Look at the notes you took on the **rhyme scheme** of the poem "The Runaway." Now, write a short poem using the same rhyme scheme as the first eight lines of "The Runaway." Each line of your poem can be short and can be about any subject you like. Remember that your **end rhymes** can be different, but your rhyme scheme must be the same.

READING FOCUS: READING A POEM

DIRECTIONS: Decide whether each of the following statements are true or false. If a statement is false, explain why.

1. Always pause at the end of a line of poetry, even if there is no punctuation.

   _____

2. When reading poetry, make a full stop for a period, comma, and colon.

   _____

3. If there is no punctuation in a poem, figure out where to pause based on the thought groups.

   _____

SKILLS FOCUS

Literary Skill
Identify and understand rhymes and rhyme schemes.

Reading Skill
Read a poem by paying careful attention to punctuation.

Collection 7

DIRECTIONS: Some of the italicized vocabulary words in the chart below are used correctly, while others are not. Use checkmarks to indicate which words are used correctly. If a word is used incorrectly, explain why and suggest a replacement.

	Correct	Incorrect
This is a brand new style that follows the latest *tradition*.		**Why?**
The movie lacked *vision* and was not very creative.		**Why?**
It was quiet in the audience because everyone had to *comment* about the speech.		**Why?**
The students all received proper *structure* in math at their new school.		**Why?**

Collection 7

LANGUAGE COACH

DIRECTIONS: Similes and metaphors are tools writers use to describe things. A **simile** compares two different things using the words *like* or *as*. A **metaphor** compares two different things, but does not use the words *like* or *as*. Complete the activity below by writing two short poems and then answering a question about what you have written.

1. Write a four-line poem about something in your life using at least two similes.

_____

_____

_____

_____

2. Rewrite your poem using metaphors instead of similes.

_____

_____

_____

_____

3. Which style suits your poem better? Why do think this is so?

_____

_____

_____

_____

ORAL LANGUAGE ACTIVITY

DIRECTIONS: How does the punctuation of a poem change the way it sounds and what it means? Take turns reading the poem "I'm Nobody" out loud with classmates. First, read the poem in a normal, conversational style. Then, read the poem and ignore all the punctuation, including question marks and exclamation points. How does the poem change? Try reading the poem and pausing for a beat or two at each punctuation mark. Which style of reading the poem works best?

Collection

8

Elements of Drama

© Michael Grimm/Getty Images

Literary and Academic Vocabulary for Collection 8

interact (IHN TUHR AKT) *v.:* act together with another.
> To understand drama, pay attention to the way characters interact.

motive (MOH TIHV) *n.:* reason someone does something.
> The character's motive for taking a vacation was to see her family.

previous (PREE VEE UHS) *adj.:* happening before a given time.
> The previous scene contained clues about how the play would end.

resolve (RIH ZAHLV) *v.:* find an answer to a problem.
> The characters resolved their problems in the final act of the play.

drama (DRAH MUH) *n.:* a story performed by actors using speech and movement.
> The theater department will be performing only one drama this season.

acts (AKTS) *n.:* sections of a play that contain related events.
> "The Monsters Are Due on Maple Street" is divided into two acts.

dialogue (DY UH LAWG) *n.:* conversation between two or more characters.
> Listen carefully to the dialogue between the husband and the wife.

stage directions (STAYJ DUH REHK SHUHNS) *n.:* directions to the actors in a script that are not meant to be spoken aloud.
> The stage directions say that the actor should walk across the stage slowly.

The Monsters Are Due on Maple Street

by Rod Serling

LITERARY FOCUS: PLOT COMPLICATIONS

In stories, **plot complications** make it hard for characters to get what they want. Usually, complications appear as soon as the characters try to get what they want, or try to solve their problems. Complications can add more conflict to the story. They also make the plot more complex. Complications are meant to increase the tension about how the story will finally end.

Find Complications   As you read Rod Serling's teleplay "The Monsters Are Due on Maple Street," keep an eye out for plot complications. What is the first plot complication that arises?

READING FOCUS: IDENTIFYING AUTHOR'S PURPOSE

People write for different **purposes**—reasons for doing something. Some common purposes include: to persuade, to inform, to entertain, to reveal a truth about life, or to share an experience. For example, a political speechwriter wants to persuade the audience to believe or do something. Newspaper reporters want to inform the reader. A person might write an action movie screenplay to entertain people.

Use the Skill   As you read "The Monsters Are Due on Maple Street," use a graphic organizer like the one below to record the purposes you think Rod Serling had for writing the teleplay. Include evidence from the text.

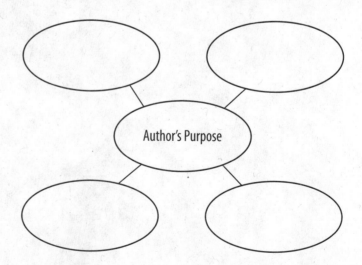

Author's Purpose

SKILLS FOCUS

Literary Skill
Recognize and understand plot complications.

Reading Skill
Identify an author's purpose.

Vocabulary Development

The Monsters Are Due on Maple Street

SELECTION VOCABULARY

transfixed (TRANS FIHKST) *v.:* used as *adj.:* very still, as if nailed to the spot.
The neighbors stood transfixed, staring at the sky.

intimidated (IHN TIHM UH DAYT IHD) *v.:* frightened, as by threats or violence.
The angry crowd intimidated the Goodmans, who began to defend themselves.

defiant (DIH FY UHNT) *adj.:* boldly resisting authority.
Those who argue with an angry crowd are defiant and courageous.

idiosyncrasy (IHD EE UH SIHNG KRUH SEE) *n.:* peculiarity; unique habit.
All people have at least one idiosyncrasy that makes them a little different.

menace (MEHN IHS) *n.:* danger, threat.
They believed that the boy was a menace to their safety.

converging (KUHN VUR JIHNG) *v.:* used as *adj.:* coming together.
The converging crowd made Tommy nervous.

WORD STUDY

DIRECTIONS: A synonym is a word with the same or almost the same meaning as another word. Each sentence below includes a word in italics that is a synonym for one of the vocabulary words above. Write the correct vocabulary word next to each sentence.

1. The dog *scared* me, so I left the area. _____

2. The mouse was *frozen* as the cat came near. _____

3. The shark was a *threat* to the swimmers. _____

4. He was *resistant* about the possibility of changing schools.

   _____

THE MONSTERS ARE DUE ON MAPLE STREET, ACT ONE

by Rod Serling

BACKGROUND

Rod Serling created *The Twilight Zone*, a hit television series that first aired in 1959. Reruns of the show can still be seen today. Serling wrote the teleplays for many episodes, including "The Monsters Are Due on Maple Street."

A **LANGUAGE COACH**

Teleplay and *screenplay* both include the word *play*, meaning "a type of performance." What do you think the prefixes *tele-* and *screen-* mean?

_____

_____

_____

_____

_____

_____

_____

Teleplay Terms

Scripts written for television or the movies are different from scripts written for the stage. A **teleplay** is a script written for TV; a **screenplay** is a script written for movies. Both kinds of scripts may contain these camera directions: **A**

fade in: The picture gradually appears on the screen.

10   **pan:** a swiveling movement of the camera, from one side to the other.

fade to black: The picture gradually disappears until all that remains is a black screen.

cut to: a sudden change from one scene or character to another.

outside shot: a camera shot of an exterior.

long shot: a camera shot from far off.

Characters

Narrator

Figure One

Figure Two

Residents of Maple Street

Steve Brand

Mrs. Brand

Don Martin

Pete Van Horn

Charlie

Charlie's wife

Tommy

Sally, Tommy's mother

Les Goodman

Mrs. Goodman

Woman Next Door

Woman One

Man One

Man Two

20   **close-up:** a camera shot that is very close to its subject.

opening shot: the first scene of the production.

dissolve: A new scene is blended with a scene that is fading out. **B**

Act One

Fade in on a shot of the night sky. The various nebulae and planets stand out in sharp, sparkling relief. As the camera begins a slow pan across the heavens, we hear the narrator offscreen.

Narrator's Voice. There is a fifth dimension beyond that which is known to man. It is a dimension as vast as space and as timeless as infinity. It is the middle ground between light and shadow—

30   between science and superstition. And it lies between the pit of man's fears and the summit of his knowledge. This is the dimension of imagination. It is an area which we call The Twilight Zone. **C** **D**

[*The camera pans down past the horizon, stopping on a sign which reads "Maple Street." Then it moves on to the street below. It is daytime. We see a quiet, tree-lined street, typical of small-town America. People sit and swing on gliders on their front porches, chatting across from house to house.* STEVE BRAND *polishes his car, while his neighbor,* DON MARTIN, *leans against the fender*

40   *watching him. A Good Humor man on a bicycle stops to sell some ice cream to a couple of kids. Two women gossip on a front lawn. Another man waters his lawn.*]

Maple Street, U.S.A., late summer. A tree-lined little world of front-porch gliders, hopscotch, the laughter of children, and the bell of an ice-cream vendor.

[*The camera moves back to the Good Humor man and the two boys who are standing alongside him, buying ice cream.*]

At the sound of the roar and the flash of light, it will be precisely 6:43 P.M. on Maple Street.

50   [*One of the boys,* TOMMY, *looks up to listen to a tremendous screeching roar from overhead. A flash of light plays on the boys' faces. It moves down the street, past lawns and porches and*

B VOCABULARY

Word Study
Identify two pairs of terms in this list that mean the opposite of each other.

_____

_____

_____

C READ AND DISCUSS

Comprehension
What's the narrator sharing with you?

D READING FOCUS

What does this description of the *Twilight Zone* suggest to you about the author's **purpose**? Is it light-hearted or serious?

_____

_____

_____

_____

_____

_____

A VOCABULARY

Selection Vocabulary

The suffix –ed is part of the word *transfixed*. What is the base word of *tranfixed*? What does it mean? What does –ed do the meaning of the word?

_____

_____

_____

_____

_____

_____

_____

B READ AND DISCUSS

Comprehension

What do the stage directions lead you to think about the roaring sound and the flashing light?

rooftops, and disappears. People leave their porches or stop what they're doing to stare up at the sky. STEVE BRAND *stops polishing his car and stands transfixed, staring upward.* **A** *He looks at* DON MARTIN, *his neighbor from across the street.*]

Steve. What was that? A meteor?

Don (*nods*). That's what it looked like. I didn't hear any crash, though, did you?

60 **Steve** (*shakes his head*). Nope. I didn't hear anything except a roar.

Mrs. Brand (*from her porch*). Steve? What was that?

Steve (*raising his voice and looking toward porch*). Guess it was a meteor, honey. Came awful close, didn't it?

Mrs. Brand. Too close for my money! Much too close.

[*People stand on their porches, watching and talking in low tones.*] **B**

Narrator's Voice. Maple Street. 6:44 P.M., on a late September evening. (*A pause*) Maple Street in the last calm and reflective moments . . . before the monsters came!

70 [*The camera pans across the porches again. A man is screwing in a lightbulb on a front porch. He gets down off the stool and flicks the switch, only to find that nothing happens. Another man is working on an electric power mower. He plugs in the plug and flicks the switch of the power mower, off and on, but nothing happens. Through the window of a front porch we see a woman at a telephone, pushing her finger back and forth on the dial hook. Her voice is indistinct and distant, but intelligible and repetitive.*]

Woman Next Door. Operator, operator, something's wrong on the phone, operator!

80 [MRS. BRAND *comes out on the porch and calls to* STEVE.]

Mrs. Brand (*calling*). Steve, the power's off. I had the soup on the stove, and the stove just stopped working.

Woman Next Door. Same thing over here. I can't get anybody on the phone either. The phone seems to be dead.

[*The camera looks down on the street. Small, mildly disturbed voices creep up from below.*]

Voices.

Electricity's off.

Phone won't work.

90   Can't get a thing on the radio.

My power mower won't move, won't work at all.

Radio's gone dead. **C**

[PETE VAN HORN, *a tall, thin man, is standing in front of his house.*]

Van Horn. I'll cut through the backyard. . . . See if the power's still on on Floral Street. I'll be right back.

[*He walks past the side of his house and disappears into the backyard. We see the hammer on his hip as he walks. The camera pans down slowly until we're looking at ten or eleven people*

100   *standing around the street and overflowing to the curb and sidewalk. In the background is* STEVE BRAND's *car.*] **D**

Steve. Doesn't make sense. Why should the power go off all of a sudden, and the phone line?

Don. Maybe some sort of an electrical storm or something.

Charlie. That don't seem likely. Sky's just as blue as anything. Not a cloud. No lightning. No thunder. No nothing. How could it be a storm?

Woman One. I can't get a thing on the radio. Not even the portable.

[*The people again murmur softly in wonderment and question.*] **E**

110   **Charlie.** Well, why don't you go downtown and check with the police, though they'll probably think we're crazy or something. A little power failure and right away we get all flustered and everything.

Steve. It isn't just the power failure, Charlie. If it was, we'd still be able to get a broadcast on the portable.

[*There's a murmur of reaction to this. Steve looks from face to face and then over to his car.*]

I'll run downtown. We'll get this all straightened out.

[STEVE *walks over to the car, gets in it, and turns the key. Through*

120   *the open car door we see the crowd watching him from the other side.* STEVE *starts the engine. It turns over sluggishly and then just stops dead. He tries it again, and this time he can't even get it to turn over. Then, very slowly and reflectively, he turns the key*

C VOCABULARY

Word Study

Some words have multiple meanings. *Dead* can mean "no longer living" as well as "no longer operating or functioning." Which definition of the word *dead* is used here?

_____

_____

_____

D LANGUAGE COACH

The word *disappears* has the **prefix** *dis–*. A prefix is a group of letters added to the beginning of a word to change its meaning. Based on how the meaning of *appears* changes when this prefix is added, what do you think *dis–* means?

_____

_____

_____

E LITERARY FOCUS

How do the people of Maple Street react to this **plot complication**?

_____

_____

_____

_____

A VOCABULARY

Word Study

When the suffix, or word ending, *–ly* is added to an adjective, it turns the word into an adverb. *Reflective* means "thoughtful." What do you think *reflectively* means?

_____

_____

_____

_____

B READ AND DISCUSS

Comprehension

What has happened?

© Louis K. Meisel Gallery, Inc./Corbis

back to "off" and slowly gets out of the car. **A** *Everyone stares at* STEVE. *He stands for a moment by the car, then walks toward the group.*]

I don't understand it. It was working fine before. . . .

Don. Out of gas?

Steve (*shakes his head*). I just had it filled up.

130   **Woman One.** What's it mean?

Charlie. It's just as if . . . as if everything had stopped. . . . (*Then he turns toward* Steve.) We'd better walk downtown.

[*Another murmur of assent at this.*]

Steve. The two of us can go, Charlie. (*He turns to look back at the car.*) It couldn't be the meteor. A meteor couldn't do this. **B**

[*He and* CHARLIE *exchange a look, then they start to walk away from the group. We see* TOMMY, *a serious-faced fourteen-year-old in spectacles, standing a few feet away from the group. He is halfway between them and the two men, who start to walk down*

140   *the sidewalk.*]

Tommy. Mr. Brand . . . you better not!

Steve. Why not?

Tommy. They don't want you to.

[STEVE *and* CHARLIE *exchange a grin, and* STEVE *looks back toward the boy.*]

Steve. Who doesn't want us to?

Tommy (*jerks his head in the general direction of the distant horizon*). Them!

Steve. Them?

150 **Charlie.** Who are them?

Tommy (*very intently*). Whoever was in that thing that came by overhead.

[STEVE *knits his brows for a moment, cocking his head questioningly. His voice is intense.*]

Steve. What?

Tommy. Whoever was in the thing that came over. I don't think they want us to leave here.

[STEVE *leaves* CHARLIE *and walks over to the boy. He kneels down in front of him. He forces his voice to remain gentle. He reaches*

160 *out and holds the boy.*]

Steve. What do you mean? What are you talking about? **C**

Tommy. They don't want us to leave. That's why they shut everything off. **D**

Steve. What makes you say that? Whatever gave you that idea?

Woman One (*from the crowd*). Now isn't that the craziest thing you ever heard?

Tommy (*persistently but a little intimidated by the crowd*). **E** It's always that way, in every story I ever read about a ship landing from outer space. **F**

170 **Woman One** (*to the boy's mother,* SALLY, *who stands on the fringe of the crowd*). From outer space, yet! Sally, you better get that boy of yours up to bed. He's been reading too many comic books or seeing too many movies or something.

Sally. Tommy, come over here and stop that kind of talk.

Steve. Go ahead, Tommy. We'll be right back. And you'll see. That wasn't any ship or anything like it. That was just a . . . a meteor or something. Likely as not— (*He turns to the group, now trying to weight his words with an optimism he obviously*

C (READING FOCUS)

What is the author's **purpose** in making Steve a patient, gentle man?

_____

_____

_____

_____

D (LITERARY FOCUS)

What possible **plot complication** is introduced by Tommy's comments?

_____

_____

_____

_____

E (VOCABULARY)

Selection Vocabulary

The word *intimidated* means "frightened with threats." Why would Tommy feel intimidated by the crowd?

_____

_____

_____

_____

F (READ AND DISCUSS)

Comprehension

What does this show you about Tommy?

A **VOCABULARY**

Selection Vocabulary

Defiant comes from the root word *defy*. What does *defy* mean?

_____

_____

_____

B **VOCABULARY**

Word Study

Based on context clues (words surrounding an unfamiliar word), what do you think *antagonism* means? Write down a definition, and then compare your definition to the one in the dictionary.

_____

_____

_____

180 *doesn't feel but is desperately trying to instill in himself, as well as the others.*) No doubt it did have something to do with all this power failure and the rest of it. Meteors can do some crazy things. Like sunspots.

Don (*picking up the cue*). Sure. That's the kind of thing—like sunspots. They raise Cain with radio reception all over the world. And this thing being so close—why, there's no telling the sort of stuff it can do. (*He wets his lips and smiles nervously.*) Go ahead, Charlie. You and Steve go into town and see if that isn't what's causing it all.

[STEVE *and* CHARLIE *walk away from the group again, down the*
190 *sidewalk. The people watch silently.* TOMMY *stares at them, biting his lips, and finally calls out again.*]

Tommy. Mr. Brand!

[*The two men stop again.* TOMMY *takes a step toward them.*]

Tommy. Mr. Brand . . . please don't leave here.

[STEVE *and* CHARLIE *stop once again and turn toward the boy. There's a murmur in the crowd, a murmur of irritation and concern as if the boy were bringing up fears that shouldn't be brought up; words that carried with them a strange kind of validity that came without logic, but nonetheless registered and had meaning and*
200 *effect.* TOMMY *is partly frightened and partly defiant.*] A

You might not even be able to get to town. It was that way in the story. Nobody could leave. Nobody except—

Steve. Except who?

Tommy. Except the people they'd sent down ahead of them. They looked just like humans. And it wasn't until the ship landed that—

[*The boy suddenly stops again, conscious of the parents staring at him and of the sudden hush of the crowd.*]

Sally (*in a whisper, sensing the antagonism of the crowd*). B
210 Tommy, please, son . . . honey, don't talk that way—

Man One. That kid shouldn't talk that way . . . and we shouldn't stand here listening to him. Why, this is the craziest thing I ever heard of. The kid tells us a comic book plot, and here we stand listening—

[STEVE *walks toward the camera and stops by the boy.*]

Steve. Go ahead, Tommy. What kind of story was this? What about the people that they sent out ahead?

Tommy. That was the way they prepared things for the landing. They sent four people. A mother and a father and two kids who
220 looked just like humans . . . but they weren't. **C**

[*There's another silence as* STEVE *looks toward the crowd and then toward* TOMMY. *He wears a tight grin.*]

Steve. Well, I guess what we'd better do then is to run a check on the neighborhood and see which ones of us are really human.

[*There's laughter at this, but it's a laughter that comes from a desperate attempt to lighten the atmosphere.* CHARLIE *laughs nervously, slightly forced. The people look at one another in the middle of their laughter.*]

Charlie. There must be somethin' better to do than stand
230 around makin' bum jokes about it. (*Rubs his jaw nervously*) I wonder if Floral Street's got the same deal we got. (*He looks past the houses.*) Where is Pete Van Horn anyway? Didn't he get back yet? **D**

[*Suddenly there's the sound of a car's engine starting to turn over. We look across the street toward the driveway of* LES GOODMAN'S *house. He's at the wheel trying to start the car.*]

Sally. Can you get it started, Les?

[LES GOODMAN *gets out of the car, shaking his head.*]

Goodman. No dice.

240 [*He walks toward the group. He stops suddenly as behind him, inexplicably and with a noise that inserts itself into the silence, the car engine starts up all by itself.* **E** GOODMAN *whirls around to stare toward it. The car idles roughly, smoke coming from the exhaust, the frame shaking gently.* GOODMAN'S *eyes go wide, and he runs over to his car. The people stare toward the car.*]

Man One. He got the car started somehow. He got his car started!

[*The camera pans along the faces of the people as they stare, somehow caught up by this revelation and somehow, illogically,*
250 *wildly, frightened.*]

C READ AND DISCUSS

Comprehension
What is on Tommy's mind?

D LITERARY FOCUS

How does not knowing what is happening on other streets add another **plot complication**?

_____
_____
_____
_____
_____
_____

E LANGUAGE COACH

If something is *explicable*, it can be explained. The **prefix** *in–* gives the word the opposite meaning. What does *inexplicably* mean here?

_____
_____
_____

A VOCABULARY

Academic Vocabulary

What is Charlie's *motive*, or reason, for saying this? How do you know?

_____

_____

_____

_____

_____

_____

_____

_____

B LANGUAGE COACH

Add the **prefix** *re–* to the word *start*. What happens to its meaning?

_____

_____

_____

_____

Woman One. How come his car just up and started like that?

Sally. All by itself. He wasn't anywheres near it. It started all by itself.

[DON *approaches the group. He stops a few feet away to look toward* GOODMAN's *car, and then back toward the group.*]

Don. And he never did come out to look at that thing that flew overhead. He wasn't even interested. (*He turns to the faces in the group, his face taut and serious.*) Why? Why didn't he come out with the rest of us to look?

260 **Charlie.** He always was an oddball. Him and his whole family. Real oddball. A

Don. What do you say we ask him?

[*The group suddenly starts toward the house. In this brief fraction of a moment they take the first step toward a metamorphosis from a group into a mob. They begin to head purposefully across the street toward the house at the end.* STEVE *stands in front of them. For a moment their fear almost turns their walk into a wild stampede, but* STEVE's *voice, loud, incisive, and commanding, makes them stop.*]

270 **Steve.** Wait a minute . . . wait a minute! Let's not be a mob!

[*The people stop as a group, seem to pause for a moment, and then much more quietly and slowly start to walk across the street.* GOODMAN *stands there alone, facing the people.*]

Goodman. I just don't understand it. I tried to start it and it wouldn't start. B You saw me. All of you saw me.

[*And now, just as suddenly as the engine started, it stops. There's a long silence that is gradually intruded upon by the frightened murmuring of the people.*]

I don't understand. I swear...I don't understand. What's

280 happening?

Don. Maybe you better tell us. Nothing's working on this street. Nothing. No lights, no power, no radio. (*And then meaningfully*) Nothing except one car—yours!

[*The people pick this up. Now their murmuring becomes a loud chant, filling the air with accusations and demands for action.*

Two of the men pass DON *and head toward* GOODMAN, *who backs away, backing into his car. He is now at bay.*]

Goodman. Wait a minute now. You keep your distance—all of you. So I've got a car that starts by itself—well, that's a freak thing, I admit it. But does that make me some kind of criminal or something? I don't know why the car works—it just does! [*This stops the crowd momentarily, and now* GOODMAN, *still backing away, goes toward his front porch. He goes up the steps and then stops to stand facing the mob.* STEVE *comes through the crowd.*]

Steve (*quietly*) We're all on a monster kick, Les. Seems that the general impression holds that maybe one family isn't what we think they are. Monsters from outer space or something. Different than us. Fifth columnists[1] from the vast beyond. (*He chuckles.*) You know anybody that might fit that description around here on Maple Street?

Goodman. What is this, a gag or something? This a practical joke or something?

[*The spotlight on his porch suddenly goes out. There's a murmur from the group.*]

Now, I suppose that's supposed to incriminate me! The light goes on and off. That really does it, doesn't it? (*He looks around the faces of the people.*) I just don't understand this— (*He wets his lips, looking from face to face.*) Look, you all know me. We've lived here five years. Right in this house. We're no different than any of the rest of you! We're no different at all. Really . . . this whole thing is just . . . just weird— **C**

Woman One. Well, if that's the case, Les Goodman, explain why— (*She stops suddenly, clamping her mouth shut.*)

Goodman (*softly*). Explain what?

Steve (*interjecting*). Look, let's forget this—

Charlie (*overlapping him*). Go ahead, let her talk. What about it? Explain what?

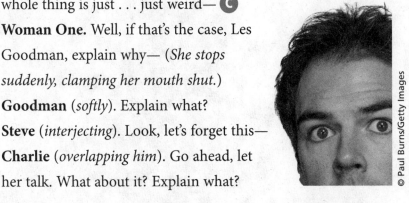
© Paul Burns/Getty Images

---

1. **fifth columnists:** people who aid an enemy from within their own country.

A **LITERARY FOCUS**

What makes the crowd's suspicion of Mr. Goodman an interesting **plot complication**?

_____

_____

_____

_____

_____

_____

_____

_____

B **READ AND DISCUSS**

Comprehension
What is the author getting at?

320 **Woman One** (*a little reluctantly*). Well . . . sometimes I go to bed late at night. A couple of times . . . a couple of times I'd come out on the porch and I'd see Mr. Goodman here in the wee hours of the morning standing out in front of his house . . . looking up at the sky. (*She looks around the circle of faces.*) That's right. Looking up at the sky as if . . . as if he were waiting for something. (*A pause*) As if he were looking for something. [*There's a murmur of reaction from the crowd again. As* GOODMAN *starts toward them, they back away, frightened.*]

Goodman. You know really . . . this is for laughs. You know

330 what I'm guilty of? (*He laughs.*) I'm guilty of insomnia. Now what's the penalty for insomnia? (*At this point the laugh, the humor, leaves his voice.*) Did you hear what I said? I said it was insomnia. (*A pause as he looks around, then shouts.*) I said it was insomnia! You fools. You scared, frightened rabbits, you. You're sick people, do you know that? You're sick people—all of you! And you don't even know what you're starting because let me tell you . . . let me tell you—this thing you're starting—that should frighten you. As God is my witness . . . you're letting something begin here that's a nightmare! **A** **B**

340 [*Fade to black.*]

THE MONSTERS ARE DUE ON MAPLE STREET, ACT TWO

by Rod Serling

BACKGROUND

When Rod Serling wrote the *Twilight Zone* episode "The Monsters Are Due on Maple Street," the United States was in the middle of the Cold War, a time of increased tension between the U.S. and the Soviet Union. Many people were afraid of the possibility of nuclear war. They even feared that communism would spread throughout the U.S. The danger of this feeling of suspicion and fear is one of the topics Serling is commenting on in this teleplay.

Act Two

Fade in on the entry hall of the Goodman house at night. On the side table rests an unlit candle. MRS. GOODMAN *walks into the scene, a glass of milk in hand. She sets the milk down on the table, lights the candle with a match from a box on the table, picks up the glass of milk, and starts out of the scene. Cut to an outside shot.* MRS. GOODMAN *comes through her porch door, glass of milk in hand. The entry hall, with the table and lit candle, can be seen behind her.* **A** *The camera slowly pans down the sidewalk, taking*

10 *in little knots of people who stand around talking in low voices. At the end of each conversation they look toward* LES GOODMAN'S *house. From the various houses we can see candlelight but no electricity. An all-pervading quiet blankets the area, disturbed only by the almost whispered voices of the people as they stand around. The camera pans over to one group where* CHARLIE *stands. He stares across at* GOODMAN'S *house. Two men stand across the street from it, in almost sentry like poses. We return to the group.*

A **READING FOCUS**

What is the **purpose** of the candles? What do they reveal about the current situation on Maple Street?

Word Study

Timorously comes from the Latin word *timor*, meaning "fear." Based on this knowledge, what tone is Sally speaking with here? Why is she speaking this way?

_____

_____

_____

_____

Word Study

Legitimate has multiple meanings. One definition of *legitimate* is "according to written law." It can also mean "of the normal kind." Which definition is used in this sentence?

_____

_____

_____

C READING FOCUS

Based on the background information on page 225, what do you think is the author's **purpose** here?

_____

_____

_____

Sally (*a little timorously*). **A** It just doesn't seem right, though, keeping watch on them. Why . . . he was right when he said he
20 was one of our neighbors. Why, I've known Ethel Goodman ever since they moved in. We've been good friends—

Charlie. That don't prove a thing. Any guy who'd spend his time lookin' up at the sky early in the morning—well there's something wrong with that kind of a person. There's something that ain't legitimate. **B** Maybe under normal circumstances we could let it go by, but these aren't normal circumstances. Why, look at this street! Nothin' but candles. Why, it's like goin' back into the dark ages or somethin'!

[STEVE *walks down the steps of his porch. He walks down the*
30 *street, over to* LES GOODMAN's *house, and stops at the foot of the steps.* GOODMAN *stands behind the screen door, his wife behind him, very frightened.*]

Goodman. Just stay right where you are, Steve. We don't want any trouble, but this time if anybody sets foot on my porch, that's what they're going to get—trouble!

Steve. Look, Les—

Goodman. I've already explained to you people. I don't sleep very well at night sometimes. I get up and I take a walk and I look up at the sky. I look at the stars!

40 **Mrs. Goodman.** That's exactly what he does. Why this whole thing, it's . . . it's some kind of madness or something.

Steve (*nods grimly*). That's exactly what it is—some kind of madness.

Charlie's Voice (*shrill, from across the street*). You best watch who you're seen with, Steve! Until we get this all straightened out, you ain't exactly above suspicion yourself. **C**

Steve (*whirling around toward him*). Or you, Charlie. Or any of us, it seems. From age eight on up!

Woman One. What I'd like to know is, what are we gonna do?
50 Just stand around here all night?

Charlie. There's nothin' else we can do! (*He turns back looking toward* STEVE *and* GOODMAN *again.*) One of 'em'll tip their hand. **D** They got to.

Steve (*raising his voice*). There's something you can do, Charlie. You could go home and keep your mouth shut. You could quit strutting around like a self-appointed hanging judge and just climb into bed and forget it.

Charlie. You sound real anxious to have that happen, Steve. I think we better keep our eye on you too!

60 **Don** (*as if he were taking the bit in his teeth, takes a hesitant step to the front*). I think everything might as well come out now. (*He turns toward* Steve.) Your wife's done plenty of talking, Steve, about how odd you are!

Charlie (*picking this up, his eyes widening*). Go ahead, tell us what she's said.

[STEVE *walks toward them from across the street.*]

Steve. Go ahead, what's my wife said? Let's get it all out. Let's pick out every idiosyncrasy of every single man, woman, and child on the street. **E** And then we might as well set up some

70 kind of a kangaroo court. How about a firing squad at dawn, Charlie, so we can get rid of all the suspects? Narrow them down. Make it easier for you.

Don. There's no need gettin' so upset, Steve. It's just that . . . well . . . Myra's talked about how there's been plenty of nights you spend hours down in your basement workin' on some kind of radio or something. Well, none of us have ever seen that radio—

[*By this time* STEVE *has reached the group. He stands there defiantly close to them.*]

Charlie. Go ahead, Steve. What kind of "radio set" you workin'

80 on? I never seen it. Neither has anyone else. Who you talk to on that radio set? And who talks to you? **F**

Steve. I'm surprised at you, Charlie. How come you're so dense all of a sudden? (*A pause*) Who do I talk to? I talk to monsters from outer space. I talk to three-headed green men who fly over here in what look like meteors.

D VOCABULARY

Word Study

Tip their hand is a figure of speech. It means "to give away a secret." Who does Charlie hope will tip their hand?

_____

_____

E VOCABULARY

Selection Vocabulary

What is a synonym for the word *idiosyncrasy*? Use a thesaurus to help you find one.

_____

F LITERARY FOCUS

What **plot complication** has just been revealed for Steve?

_____

_____

_____

_____

_____

_____

Selection Vocabulary

What word does the author contrast with *menace* in this sentence? What clue does this give you to the meaning of *menace*?

_____

_____

_____

_____

_____

B READING FOCUS

The author **reveals a truth** about human nature here. What is it?

_____

_____

_____

_____

_____

_____

_____

[STEVE's *wife steps down from their porch, bites her lip, calls out.*]

Mrs. Brand. Steve! Steve, please. (*Then looking around, frightened, she walks toward the group.*) It's just a ham radio set, that's all. I bought him a book on it myself. It's just a ham radio

90 set. A lot of people have them. I can show it to you. It's right down in the basement.

Steve. (*whirls around toward her*). Show them nothing! If they want to look inside our house—let them get a search warrant.

Charlie. Look, buddy, you can't afford to—

Steve (*interrupting*). Charlie, don't tell me what I can afford! And stop telling me who's dangerous and who isn't and who's safe and who's a menace. **A** (*He turns to the group and shouts.*) And you're with him too—all of you! You're standing here all set to crucify—all set to find a scapegoat—all desperate to point some

100 kind of a finger at a neighbor! Well now look, friends, the only thing that's gonna happen is that we'll eat each other up alive. **B**

[*He stops abruptly as* CHARLIE *suddenly grabs his arm.*]

Charlie (*in a hushed voice*). That's not the only thing that can happen to us. **C**

[*Cut to a long shot looking down the street. A figure has suddenly materialized in the gloom, and in the silence we can hear the clickety clack of slow, measured footsteps on concrete as the figure, walks slowly toward them. One of the women lets out a stifled cry. The young mother grabs her boy, as do a couple of others.*]

110 **Tommy** (*shouting, frightened*). It's the monster! It's the monster!

[*Another woman lets out a wail and the people fall back in a group, staring toward the darkness and the approaching figure. As the people stand in the shadows watching,* DON MARTIN *joins them, carrying a shot-gun. He holds it up.*]

Don. We may need this.

Steve. A shotgun? (*He pulls it out of* DON's *hand.*) Good Lord— will anybody think a thought around here? Will you people wise up? What good would a shotgun do against—

[*Now* CHARLIE *pulls the gun from* STEVE's *hand.*]

120   **Charlie.** No more talk, Steve. You're going to talk us into a grave! You'd let whatever's out there walk right over us, wouldn't yuh? Well, some of us won't!

[*He swings the gun around to point it toward the sidewalk. The dark figure continues to walk toward them. The group stands there, fearful, apprehensive.* **D** *Mothers clutch children, men stand in front of wives.* CHARLIE *slowly raises the gun. As the figure gets closer and closer, he suddenly pulls the trigger. The sound of it explodes in the stillness. The figure suddenly lets out a small cry, stumbles forward onto his knees, and then falls*

130   *forward on his face.* DON, CHARLIE, *and* STEVE *race over to him.* STEVE *is there first and turns the man over. Now the crowd gathers around them.*]

  Steve (*slowly looks up*). It's Pete Van Horn.

  Don (*in a hushed voice*). Pete Van Horn! He was just gonna go over to the next block to see if the power was on.

  Woman One. You killed him, Charlie. You shot him dead!

  Charlie (*looks around at the circle of faces, his eyes frightened, his face contorted*). But . . . but I didn't know who he was. I certainly didn't know who he was. He comes walkin' out of the

140   darkness—how am I supposed to know who he was? (*He grabs* STEVE.) Steve—you know why I shot! How was I supposed to know he wasn't a monster or something? (*He grabs* DON *now.*) We're all scared of the same thing. I was just tryin' to . . . tryin' to protect my home, that's all! Look, all of you, that's all I was tryin' to do. (*He looks down wildly at the body.*) I didn't know it was somebody we knew! I didn't know— **E**

[*There's a sudden hush and then an intake of breath. We see the living room window of* CHARLIE's *house. The window is not lit, but suddenly the house lights come on behind it.*]

150   **Woman One** (*in a very hushed voice*). Charlie . . . Charlie . . . the lights just went on in your house. Why did the lights just go on?

  Don. What about it, Charlie? How come you're the only one with lights now?

D   **VOCABULARY**

Word Study
What simpler word does the author pair with the word *apprehensive*? How does this help you understand the meaning of *apprehensive*?

_____

_____

_____

_____

E   **READ AND DISCUSS**

Comprehension
What is Charlie's motive for his actions?

_____

_____

_____

_____

_____

_____

_____

_____

_____

Word Study

Gag is a synonym for *joke* in this context. What is another meaning of the word *gag*? Would that definition make sense here?

_____

_____

_____

_____

_____

_____

Goodman. That's what I'd like to know.

[*There is a pause as they all stare toward* CHARLIE.]

You were so quick to kill, Charlie, and you were so quick to tell us who we had to be careful of. Well, maybe you had to kill. Maybe Peter there was trying to tell us something. Maybe he'd found out something and came back to tell us who there was

160 amongst us we should watch out for—

[CHARLIE *backs away from the group, his eyes wide with fright.*]

Charlie. No . . . no . . . it's nothing of the sort! I don't know why the lights are on. I swear I don't. Somebody's pulling a gag or something. A

[*He bumps against* STEVE, *who grabs him and whirls him around.*]

Steve. A gag? A gag? Charlie, there's a dead man on the sidewalk and you killed him! Does this thing look like a gag to you? B

[CHARLIE *breaks away and screams as he runs toward his house.*]

170 **Charlie**. No! No! Please!

[*A man breaks away from the crowd to chase* CHARLIE. *The man tackles him and lands on top of him. The other people start to run toward them.* CHARLIE *is up on his feet. He breaks away from the other man's grasp and lands a couple of desperate punches that push the man aside. Then he forces his way, fighting, through the crowd to once again break free. He jumps up on his front porch. A rock thrown from the group smashes a window alongside of him, the broken glass flying past him. A couple of pieces cut him. He stands there perspiring, rumpled, blood running down from*

180 *a cut on his cheek. His wife breaks away from the group to throw herself into his arms. He buries his face against her. We can see the crowd converging on the porch now.*]

Voices.

It must have been him. He's the one.

We got to get Charlie.

[*Another rock lands on the porch. Now* CHARLIE *pushes his wife behind him, facing the group.*]

Charlie. Look, look, I swear to you . . . it isn't me . . . but I do know who it is . . . I swear to you, I do know who it is. I know
190   who the monster is here. I know who it is that doesn't belong. I swear to you I know.

Goodman (*shouting*). What are you waiting for?

Woman One (*shouting*). Come on, Charlie, come on.

Man One (*shouting*). Who is it, Charlie, tell us!

Don (*pushing his way to the front of the crowd*). All right, Charlie, let's hear it!

[CHARLIE's *eyes dart around wildly.*]

Charlie. It's . . . it's . . .

Man Two (*screaming*). Go ahead, Charlie, tell us.

200   **Charlie.** It's . . . it's the kid. It's Tommy. He's the one. **C**

[*There's a gasp from the crowd as we cut to a shot of the mother holding her boy. The boy at first doesn't understand. Then, realizing the eyes are all on him, he buries his face against his mother,* SALLY.]

Sally (*backs away*). That's crazy. That's crazy. He's a little boy.

Woman One. But he knew! He was the only one who knew! He told us all about it. Well, how did he know? How could he have known?

[*The various people take this up and repeat the questions aloud.*]

210   **Voices.**

How could he know? Who told him?

Make the kid answer.

Man One. What about Goodman's car?

Don. It was Charlie who killed old man Van Horn.

Woman One. But it was the kid here who knew what was going to happen all the time. He was the one who knew!

[STEVE *shouts at his hysterical neighbors.*]

Steve. Are you all gone crazy? (*Pause as he looks about*) Stop.

[*A fist crashes at* STEVE's *face, staggering him back out of view.*
220   *Several close camera shots suggest the coming of violence: A hand fires a rifle. A fist clenches. A hand grabs the hammer from* VAN HORN's *body, etc.*]

Don. Charlie has to be the one—Where's my rifle?

C READING FOCUS

Based on what you have read so far, what do you think is the author's **purpose** or purposes for writing this teleplay? Was it to persuade, inform, entertain, reveal a truth about life, or share an experience? Explain your answer.

_____

_____

_____

_____

_____

_____

_____

_____

_____

_____

_____

_____

_____

_____

_____

_____

_____

A **LITERARY FOCUS**

What is the final **plot complication** that the people of Maple Street face?

_____

_____

_____

_____

_____

_____

B **READING FOCUS**

What was the author's **purpose** for having the camera move back and forth?

_____

_____

_____

_____

_____

_____

Woman One. Les Goodman's the one. His car started! Let's wreck it.

Mrs. Goodman. What about Steve's radio—He's the one that called them

Mr. Goodman.' Smash the radio. Get me a hammer. Get me something.

230 **Steve.** Stop—Stop

Charlie. Where's that kid—Let's get him.

Man One. Get Steve—Get Charlie—They're working together. [_The crowd starts to converge around the mother, who grabs her son and starts to run with him. The crowd starts to follow, at first, walking fast, and then running after him. Suddenly,_ CHARLIE's _lights go off and the lights in another house go on. They stay on for a moment, then from across the street other lights go on and then off again._]

Man One (_shouting_). It isn't the kid. . . . It's Bob Weaver's house.

240 **Woman One.** It isn't Bob Weaver's house, it's Don Martin's place.

Charlie. I tell you, it's the kid.

Don. It's Charlie. He's the one. **A**

[_The people shout, accuse, scream. The camera tilts back and forth._ **B** _We see panic-stricken faces in close-up and tilting shots of houses as the lights go on and off Slowly, in the middle of this nightmarish morass of sight and sound, the camera starts to pull away, until once again we've reached the opening shot, looking at the Maple Street sign from high above. The camera continues to move away until we dissolve to a shot of the metal side of a_

250 _spacecraft, which sits shrouded in darkness. An open door throws out a beam of light from the illuminated interior. Two figures silhouetted against the bright lights appear. We get only a vague feeling of form, but nothing more explicit than that._] **C**

Figure One. Understand the procedure now? Just stop a few of their machines and radios and telephones and lawn mowers . . . throw them into darkness for a few hours and then you just sit back and watch the pattern.

Figure Two. And this pattern is always the same?

© McPherson Colin/Corbis Sygma

D **LITERARY FOCUS**

Who are these figures? What does their conversation tell you about their role in the story's **plot complications**?

_____
_____
_____
_____
_____
_____

Figure One. With few variations. They pick the most dangerous enemy they can find . . . and it's themselves. And all we need do is sit back . . . and watch.

Figure Two. Then I take it this place . . . this Maple Street . . . is not unique.

Figure One (*shaking his head*). By no means. Their world is full of Maple Streets. And we'll go from one to the other and let them destroy themselves. One to the other . . . one to the other . . . one to the other— **D**

[*Now the camera pans up for a shot of the starry sky.*]

Narrator's Voice. The tools of conquest do not necessarily come with bombs and explosions and fallout. There are weapons that are simply thoughts, attitudes, prejudices—to be found only in the minds of men. For the record, prejudices can kill and suspicion can destroy, and a thoughtless, frightened search for a scapegoat has a fallout all of its own for the children . . . the children yet unborn. (*A pause*) And the pity of it is . . . that these things cannot be confined to . . . The Twilight Zone! **E**

[*Fade to black.*]

E **READING FOCUS**

What do the final words of the narrator **reveal** to you about the author's **purpose** for this story?

_____
_____
_____
_____
_____
_____
_____
_____
_____
_____
_____
_____

The Monsters Are Due on Maple Street, Act One

USE A CAUSE-AND-EFFECT CHART

It can be helpful to keep track of **plot complications** in a story using a cause-and-effect chart. In the graphic organizer below, write down four major events or plot complications in the left column. In the right column, describe the effects, or results, of those events and complications.

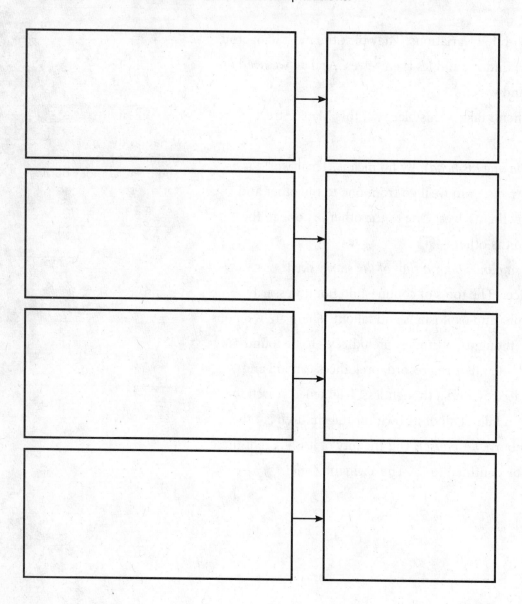

Applying Your Skills

The Monsters Are Due on Maple Street

VOCABULARY DEVELOPMENT

DIRECTIONS: Write the vocabulary words from the Word Box on the correct blanks to complete each sentence. One word will not be used.

Word Box

transfixed

intimidated

defiant

idiosyncrasy

menace

converging

1. When something strange flew overhead, people on the street stood _____ as they watched it.

2. Sally spoke softly because she was _____ by the angry crowd.

3. Tommy explained an evil _____ he had read about in a science fiction story.

4. Goodman was angry and _____ in the face of the mob.

5. The crowd, _____ on Charlie after he shoots Pete, was angry and confused.

LITERARY FOCUS: PLOT COMPLICATIONS

DIRECTIONS: Answer the following questions about **plot complications** in "The Monsters Are Due on Maple Street" on a separate sheet of paper.

1. What do you think is the first plot complication in the story?

2. What do the people on Maple Street want to do before this complication?

3. What do they want afterwards?

4. Which plot complication do you think created the most tension and suspense in the story? Why?

READING FOCUS: IDENTIFYING AUTHOR'S PURPOSE

DIRECTIONS: Study the notes you took for "The Monsters Are Due on Maple Street." On a separate sheet of paper, write a short paragraph explaining why you think Rod Serling ended the teleplay the way he did. What was his **purpose** in telling this story with this ending?

SKILLS FOCUS

Literary Skill
Recognize and understand plot complications.

Reading Skill
Identify an author's purpose.

Collection 8

VOCABULARY REVIEW

DIRECTIONS: In each of the sentences below, circle the word or phrase that means the same thing as the italicized vocabulary word.

1. She was determined to *resolve* the issue, noting that someone must be able to fix the problem.

2. He thought about the *previous* day's activity, reflecting on the fun things he had done the day before.

3. On the final lap, the other racers closed in, *converging* on the leader as he neared the finish line.

4. The car had many peculiarities, but this was the first time John had noticed this particular *idiosyncrasy*.

5. He had to warn the divers about the *menace* of the shark, which was the greatest danger facing them.

DIRECTIONS: In each of the sentences below, circle the word or phrase that means the opposite, of the italicized vocabulary word.

1. Sally sprang into action while Josh stood *transfixed* by the terrible sound.

2. Any story I write in the future will take place in the Wild West, because all my *previous* stories took place in boring locations.

3. But, officer, I had no reason to steal the diamond, so what's my *motive*?

4. Instead of being *intimidated* by the pack, the little dog bravely stood his ground.

5. As everyone else followed the order to get into line, Tom remained *defiant*, staying at his desk.

Skills Review

Collection 8

LANGUAGE COACH

DIRECTIONS: Many words are formed by adding a **prefix** such as *un–* or *re–* to a base word. For example, adding *un–* to *believable* makes the word *unbelievable*, the opposite of *believable*. Adding *re–* to *start* makes *restart*, or "to start again." Think of three words to which you can add one of these two prefixes. Write them with prefixes attached on the lines below, along with their new meanings.

1. _____
2. _____
3. _____

DIRECTIONS: The base word *wind* (WYND) can take both prefixes, *un–* and *re–*. First, write the meaning of the base word. Then, add each prefix individually and write the meanings of the new words.

4. _____
5. _____
6. _____

WRITING ACTIVITY

DIRECTIONS: On a separate sheet of paper, write a few sentences that describe a different ending for "The Monsters Are Due on Maple Street." For example, what if the aliens reveal themselves to the neighbors? What if there really was an alien spy on Maple Street? Then, write a brief paragraph explaining how your different ending would or would not change the **purpose** of writer Rod Serling's original teleplay. In other words, does the play have the same purpose with your ending as it did with the original ending? Why or why not?

Collection
9
Greek Myths and World Folk Tales

© Orpheus and Eurydice (gouache on paper),
McBride, Angus/Private Collection, © Look and
Learn/The Bridgeman Art Library International

Literary and Academic Vocabulary for Collection 9

---

classic (KLAS IHK) *adj.:* well-known, especially as being traditional or typical.
The story of King Midas is a classic myth.

foundation (FOWN DAY SHUHN) *n.:* basis; idea, fact, or system from which something develops.
Many ancient myths provided a foundation for understanding the world.

generation (JEHN UH RAY SHUHN) *n.:* all the people in a society or family who are about the same age.
Folk tales are often passed down from a previous generation.

intervene (IHN TUHR VEEN) *v.:* to do something to try to stop an argument or solve a problem.
Sometimes in a myth, a powerful force will intervene on behalf of humans.

myth (MIHTH) *n.:* story that represents the deepest wishes and fears of human beings, used by ancient peoples to explain the mysterious and frightening forces of the universe.
The myth explained why storms and floods took place.

moral (MAWR UHL) *n.:* lesson about the right way to behave.
The moral of the story was to obey your parents.

Preparing to Read

Orpheus, the Great Musician

retold by Olivia Coolidge

LITERARY FOCUS: THE UNDERWORLD OF MYTH

Myths are stories that represent the deepest wishes and fears of human beings. In ancient Greek myths, the **underworld** is a dark and gloomy place ruled by the god Hades. Normally, only the souls of the dead go to the underworld. Sometimes, however, living people attempt the dangerous journey, usually to reach someone who has died.

Identify Elements of the Underworld As you read "Orpheus, the Great Musician," look for passages that describe the underworld and what it represents. What role does the underworld play in the story?

READING FOCUS: SUMMARIZING

When you **summarize**, you mention only the most important information in a text. This information can include the title, author, main characters, conflict (struggle or problem), main events, and resolution (how the story ends).

Use the Skill As you read "Orpheus, the Great Musician," summarize the myth. Who are the main characters? What is the main conflict? What events happen in the story? How does it end? Use a chart like this one to take notes before you summarize:

Summarizing a Myth	"Notes from Your Reading"
Title	"Orpheus, the Great Musician"
Author	Ancient Greeks, retold by Olivia Coolidge
Main characters	Orpheus
Conflict	
Main events	
Resolution	

SKILLS FOCUS

Literary Skill
Identify and understand elements of myth: the underworld.

Reading Skill
Summarize a text.

Vocabulary Development

Orpheus, the Great Musician

SELECTION VOCABULARY

inconsolabe (IHN KUHN SOH LUH BUHL) *adj.:* unable to be comforted; brokenhearted.

Orpheus is inconsolable when his true love dies.

instinct (IHN STIHNGKT) *n.:* inborn pattern of behavior.

Orpheus uses instinct to determine if his true love is near.

reluctance (RIH LUHK TUHNS) *n.:* unwillingness.

His reluctance to live without his love led Orpheus to the underworld.

unfortunate (UHN FAWR CHUH NIHT) *adj.:* marked by ill fortune.

Orpheus is unfortunate in matters of love.

WORD STUDY

DIRECTIONS: Certain prefixes can change the meaning of a word. Often, this gives the new word the opposite meaning of the root word, particularly when the prefixes *in–* or *un–* are used. For example, *incorrect* means the opposite of *correct*. Not all words that start with *in* use prefixes, however. *Instinct* is a word on its own (*stinct* is not a word). What two words on the list above are created by adding prefixes to existing words?

1. _____

2. _____

What are their root words and what do the root words mean?

3. _____

4. _____

ORPHEUS, THE GREAT MUSICIAN

retold by Olivia Coolidge

BACKGROUND

This ancient Greek myth describes a journey to the underworld. Orpheus traveled there to try to save Eurydice, whom he loved. According to the beliefs of the ancient Greeks, to reach the underworld, a person had to cross the River Styx (STIKS) on a ferryboat rowed by a man named Charon (KER UHN), then pass through gates guarded by Cerberus (SUR BUHR UHS), a three-headed dog. Olivia Coolidge based this story on the old Greek myths. She retold an ancient story for a modern audience.

A **READ AND DISCUSS**

Comprehension

What does this information about wild beasts, trees, and rocks tell you about Orpheus?

In the legend of Orpheus, the Greek love of music found its fullest expression. Orpheus, it is said, could make such heavenly songs that when he sat down to sing, the trees would crowd around to shade him. The ivy and vine stretched out their tendrils. Great oaks would bend their spreading branches over his head. The very rocks would edge down the mountainsides. Wild beasts crouched harmless by him, and nymphs[1] and woodland gods would listen to him, enchanted. **A**

10 Orpheus himself, however, had eyes for no one but the nymph Eurydice.[2] His love for her was his inspiration, and his power sprang from the passionate longing that he knew in his own heart. All nature rejoiced with him on his bridal day, but on that very morning, as Eurydice went down to the riverside with her maidens to gather flowers for a bridal garland, she was bitten in the foot by a snake, and she died in spite of all attempts to save her.

---

1. **nymphs:** minor goddesses of nature, usually young and beautiful, living in mountains, rivers, or trees.
2. **Eurydice** (YOO RIHD UH SEE)

Orpheus was inconsolable. All day long he mourned his bride, while birds, beasts, and the earth itself sorrowed with him. When at last the shadows of the sun grew long, Orpheus took his lyre[3] and made his way to the yawning cave which leads down into the underworld, where the soul of dead Eurydice had gone.

Even gray Charon, the ferryman of the Styx, forgot to ask his passenger for the price of crossing. The dog Cerberus, the three-headed monster who guards Hades' gate, stopped full in his tracks and listened motionless until Orpheus had passed. **B** As he entered the land of Hades, the pale ghosts came after him like great, uncounted flocks of silent birds. All the land lay hushed as that marvelous voice resounded across the mud and marshes of its dreadful rivers. In the daffodil fields of Elysium, the happy dead sat silent among their flowers. In the farthest corners of the place of punishment, the hissing flames stood still. Accursed Sisyphus,[4] who toils eternally to push a mighty rock uphill, sat down and knew not he was resting. Tantalus, who strains forever after visions of cool water, forgot his thirst and ceased to clutch at the empty air. **C D**

The pillared[5] hall of Hades opened before the hero's song. The ranks of long-dead heroes who sit at Hades' board looked up

© Erich Lessing/Art Resource, NY

---

3. **lyre** (LYR): small harp.
4. **Sisyphus** (SIHS UH FUHS)
5. **pillared:** having pillars, or columns.

B **LANGUAGE COACH**

Many words in this sentence have **suffixes,** or word endings attached to them. List four of these words and underline their suffixes.

_____

_____

_____

_____

C **LITERARY FOCUS**

How is the **underworld** described in this paragraph?

_____

_____

_____

_____

_____

_____

_____

_____

_____

D **READ AND DISCUSS**

Comprehension

How has Orpheus's singing been affected by Eurydice's death so far?

A **READING FOCUS**

Summarize who and what Orpheus encounters on his journey.

_____

_____

_____

_____

_____

_____

B **READ AND DISCUSS**

Comprehension

Why might Orpheus believe that Hades might trick him?

C **LITERARY FOCUS**

How is Orpheus's trip out of the **underworld** different from his journey to the underworld?

_____

_____

_____

_____

D **VOCABULARY**

Selection Vocabulary

Instinct means "inborn pattern of behavior." Use the word in a sentence of your own.

_____

_____

_____

and turned their eyes away from the pitiless form of Hades and his pale, unhappy queen. Grim and unmoving sat the dark king of the dead on his ebony throne, yet the tears shone on his rigid
40 cheeks in the light of his ghastly torches. Even his hard heart, which knew all misery and cared nothing for it, was touched by the love and longing of the music. **A**

At last the minstrel[6] came to an end, and a long sigh like wind in pine trees was heard from the assembled ghosts. Then the king spoke, and his deep voice echoed through his silent land. "Go back to the light of day," he said. "Go quickly while my monsters are stilled by your song. Climb up the steep road to daylight, and never once turn back. The spirit of Eurydice shall follow, but if you look around at her, she will return to me."

50 Orpheus turned and strode from the hall of Hades, and the flocks of following ghosts made way for him to pass. In vain he searched their ranks for a sight of his lost Eurydice. In vain he listened for the faintest sound behind. The barge of Charon sank to the very gunwales[7] beneath his weight, but no following passenger pressed it lower down. The way from the land of Hades to the upper world is long and hard, far easier to descend than climb. It was dark and misty, full of strange shapes and noises, yet in many places merely black and silent as the tomb. Here Orpheus would stop and listen, but nothing moved behind
60 him. For all he could hear, he was utterly alone. Then he would wonder if the pitiless Hades were deceiving him. Suppose he came up to the light again and Eurydice was not there! Once he had charmed the ferryman and the dreadful monsters, but now they had heard his song. The second time his spell would be less powerful; he could never go again. Perhaps he had lost Eurydice by his readiness to believe. **B C**

Every step he took, some instinct told him that he was going farther from his bride. **D** He toiled up the path in reluctance and despair, stopping, listening, sighing, taking a few slow steps, until

---

6. **minstrel:** singer.
7. **gunwales** (GUHN UHLZ): upper edges of the sides of a boat.

70   the dark thinned out into grayness. **E** Up ahead a speck of light showed clearly the entrance to the cavern.

At that final moment Orpheus could bear no more. To go out into the light of day without his love seemed to him impossible. Before he had quite ascended, there was still a moment in which he could go back. Quick in the grayness he turned and saw a dim shade at his heels, as indistinct as the gray mist behind her. But still he could see the look of sadness on her face as he sprung forward saying, "Eurydice!" and threw his arms about her. The shade dissolved in the circle of his arms like smoke. A little whisper seemed
80   to say "Farewell" as she scattered into mist and was gone.

The unfortunate lover hastened back again down the steep, dark path. But all was in vain. This time the ghostly ferryman was deaf to his prayers. The very wildness of his mood made it impossible for him to attain the beauty of his former music. At last, his despair was so great that he could not even sing at all. **F** For seven days he sat huddled together on the gray mud banks, listening to the wailing of the terrible river. The flitting ghosts shrank back in a wide circle from the living man, but he paid them no attention. Only he sat with his eyes on Charon, his ears
90   ringing with the dreadful noise of Styx. **G**

Orpheus arose at last and stumbled back along the steep road he knew so well by now. When he came up to earth again, his song was pitiful but more beautiful than ever. Even the nightingale who mourned all night long would hush her voice to listen as Orpheus sat in some hidden place singing of his lost Eurydice. Men and women he could bear no longer, and when they came to hear him, he drove them away. At last the women of Thrace, maddened by Dionysus and infuriated by Orpheus's contempt, fell upon him and killed him. It is said that as the body was swept
100 down the river Hebrus, the dead lips still moved faintly and the rocks echoed for the last time, "Eurydice." But the poet's eager spirit was already far down the familiar path.

In the daffodil meadows he met the shade of Eurydice, and there they walk together, or where the path is narrow, the shade of Orpheus goes ahead and looks back at his love. **H**

E VOCABULARY

Selection Vocabulary

Reluctance comes from the Latin word *reluctari*, "to struggle against." What is Orpheus "struggling against" in this paragraph?

_____

_____

F VOCABULARY

Academic Vocabulary

What is the *foundation*, or basis, of Orpheus's grief?

_____

_____

_____

_____

G READING FOCUS

Summarize what happens after Orpheus turns back to look for Eurydice.

_____

_____

_____

_____

_____

H READ AND DISCUSS

Comprehension

How did Orpheus live his final days?

Orpheus, the Great Musician

USE A CONCEPT WEB

DIRECTIONS: Many myths include events that seem incredible or extraordinary. In other words, things happen in myths that we do not see in everyday life. People have amazing powers or travel to strange places. There are several fantastic events in "Orpheus, the Great Musician." Use the diagram below to list four of these events.

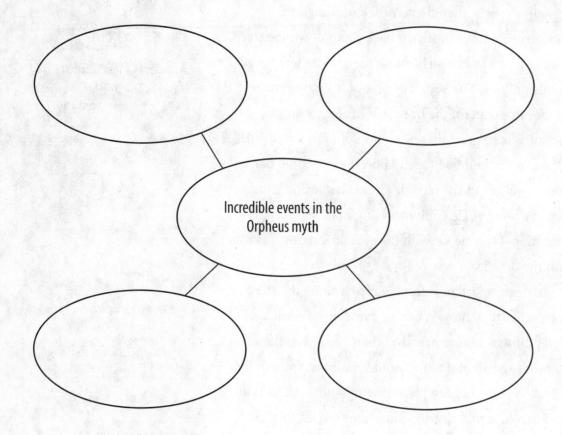

Incredible events in the Orpheus myth

Applying Your Skills

Orpheus, the Great Musician

VOCABULARY DEVELOPMENT

DIRECTIONS: Write the vocabulary words from the Word Box on the correct blanks to complete the sentences below.

Word Box

inconsolable

instinct

reluctance

unfortunate

1. John was _____ after his pet died.

2. Losing the winning lottery ticket was a very _____ event.

3. The puppy showed great _____ to enter the kennel because he was afraid of the other dogs.

4. Juan reacted out of pure _____, catching the ball without even thinking.

LITERARY FOCUS: THE UNDERWORLD OF MYTH

DIRECTIONS: Fill in the following table with descriptions of the **underworld** from "Orpheus, the Great Musician."

The Underworld	
What does it look like?	
What kind of place is it?	
Who does Orpheus meet there?	

READING FOCUS: SUMMARIZING

DIRECTIONS: Study the **summary** chart that you made as you read this myth. Use it to answer the following questions on a separate sheet of paper.

1. Who are the main characters of the myth?

2. Why does Orpheus go to the underworld?

3. What happens in the underworld? How does Orpheus react?

4. What happens to Orpheus after he returns home?

SKILLS FOCUS

Literary Skill
Identify and understand elements of myth: the underworld.

Reading Skills
Summarize a text.

Skills Review

Collection 9

VOCABULARY REVIEW

DIRECTIONS: In the paragraph below, fill in each blank with the correct vocabulary word from the Word Box.

Word Box

classic
foundation
generation
inconsolable
instinct
intervene
reluctance
unfortunate

The story of Orpheus and Eurydice is a (1) _____ myth. The story has passed from one (2) _____ to the next. In spite of the (3) _____ fate of Orpheus, the myth remains popular. The ancient Greek belief in the underworld provided a (4) _____ for understanding what happens when people die. Orpheus becomes heartbroken and (5) _____ over Eurydice's death. He is determined to (6) _____ in the affairs of the gods and demand the return of Eurydice. Orpheus overcomes his (7) _____ and fear, and makes the journey to the underworld. However, his (8) _____ tells him that Eurydice is not behind him when he leaves the underworld.

DIRECTIONS: Match each vocabulary word in the left column with the word or phrase in the right column that means the opposite.

_____ 1. classic   a. lucky
_____ 2. inconsolable   b. eagerness
_____ 3. unfortunate   c. leave alone
_____ 4. reluctance   d. new
_____ 5. intervene   e. joyful

Skills Review

Collection 9

LANGUAGE COACH

DIRECTIONS: Recall that **suffixes** are word parts added to the end of words. Suffixes often change a word's part of speech and its definition. Add the suffix in the second column to the vocabulary word in the first column, and then complete the rest of the chart. You can use a dictionary if you need help.

Vocabulary word	Suffix added	New word	Part of speech of new word	Definition of new word
myth	-ical			
unfortunate	-ly			
intervene	-tion			
moral	-ity			
instinct	-ual			

WRITING ACTIVITY

Write the opening paragraph of your own **myth**. Think of an interesting question that someone might have about the world around them, such as Why there are rainbows?, What are stars?, or How do the seasons change? Your myth will be a story that answers that question, although you only need to write the beginning of the myth. You should make the subject of your myth clear in your paragraph. Use one of the following academic vocabulary words in your paragraph: *classic, foundation, generation,* or *intervene.*

Index of Authors and Titles